Rathlin Island

North of Antrim

Hugh Alexander Boyd

Clachan
Publishing

Rathlin Island

North of Antrim

Hugh Alexander Boyd

6 Hillside Road, Ballycastle,
Glens of Antrim, Northern Ireland.

Email: clachanpublishing@outlook.com

Website: https://www.clachanbooks.com
ISBN — 978-1-909906-65-5

This edition published 2025
Original edition published 1947

Church Pier, Quay and Manor House

Rathlin Island

NORTH OF ANTRIM

by

Hugh Alexander Boyd

§

First printed and published by
J. S. SCARLETT @ SON
BALLYCASTLE, Northern Ireland

July, 1947.

*This reformatted edition has endeavoured to retain many of the features of the original.
Cover design based on original cover by*

In Memory

of

COLONEL ALAN JAMES CAMPBELL,

Indian Army,

Companion of the Distinguished Service Order,

Married in St. Thomas's Parish Church,

Rathlin,

11th August, 1897,

Died 16th October, 1944, in his eightieth year,

a verray parfit gentil knyght

whose quiet bearing and gallant personality

reflected the qualities of the

Christian Soldier.

FOREWORD

BY

PROFESSOR E. ESTYN EVANS, M.A., D.Sc.,

Fellow of the Society of Antiquaries,
Member of the Royal Irish Academy,
Professor of Geography in the Queen's University, Belfast.

A visit to Rathlin Island is an experience never to be forgotten, and there are many who, having once made the journey, will be tempted back again and again. This little book will give the visitor a foretaste of the riches he may expect to discover across the tide-ripped Sound. In Rathlin he will not only find peace and the friendship of a sturdy, intelligent and resourceful people, but he will be given the freedom of a miniature kingdom which he can traverse from end to end in the course of a long summer's day.

Geologically youthful, it is an island old in human experience. To the archaeologist, the geographer, the artist, the ethnologist, the botanist or bird-watcher, Rathlin is an earthly paradise; and Mr. Boyd has set out some of its attractions in the following pages. He has also given sources for further reading which the student can follow up at leisure, and he has re-printed for the benefit of ornithologists Mr. Robert Patterson's authoritative list of the "Birds of Rathlin Island "from *The Irish Naturalist*.

If Ballycastle is fortunate in having such wealth at its doors, it is fortunate also in having one of its own sons to unfold the colourful record of its past. The scenic heritage and historic monuments of Ulster would be made safe for future generations if every region had its devoted historian and topographer to do for it what Mr. Boyd is doing for his native district. I wish his little book every success.

E. ESTYN EVANS.

Queen's University, Belfast.
19 : vi. :1947.

PREFACE.

Rathlin Island is visited yearly by an increasingly large number of visitors from all parts of the British Isles. It is because I am emboldened to think that they may care to read something of its history that I have compiled the following pages. This booklet makes no claim whatever to be anything more than the briefest outline of the story of the island. The present high cost of printing has precluded the incorporation of material that otherwise might have been included. I hope I have rightly assumed that it was better to produce a short account of the island and at a reasonable cost than to attempt a more detailed study, the cost of which would have been likely to have given it a much more restricted appeal. To those who may be sufficiently interested to pursue the study of Rathlin in greater detail the Bibliography (which does not pretend to be exhaustive) may at least provide some helpful and informative "leads."

I should like to thank Professor E. E. Evans, first occupant of the recently established Chair of Geography in the Queen's University, Belfast, for the high honour he has done me by writing the Foreword. In the excellent work that is being accomplished by Professor Evans's Department, the town and ordinary townsman are associated with the gown and groves of academus in a manner that is unfortunately all too rare in many of our seats of learning. I have also to thank Mr. K. C. Edwards, M.A., F.R.G.S., a visitor to these parts, for the map which he kindly prepared for me in his Department of Geography, University College, Nottingham. To Mr. George W. Scarlett of the firm of Messrs. J. S. Scarlett & Son, I am specially indebted. His enterprise has not only made possible the appearance of the booklet, but his skill and resourcefulness have combined to produce a most creditable specimen of provincial printing.

HUGH ALEXANDER BOYD.

Islandview, Cushendall Road,
    Ballycastle, 19th June, 1947.

CONTENTS.

	PAGE
Introductory - - - -	11
Early History - - - -	15
Mediaeval Times - - - -	25
The Gage Family - - - -	30
A Question of Language - - -	40
Later History - - - -	49
The Present Day - - - -	58
The Enchanted Isle - - - -	63
Bibliography - - - -	65
The Birds of Rathlin Island - - -	67

Illustrations.

Church Pier, Quay & Manor – House	*Frontispiece*
Rathlin East Lighthouse - -	18
St. Thomas Parish Church - -	36
Chapel of the Immaculate Conception	50
Birds on Rocks at West Lighthouse- -	64
Map - - - - -	72

Cover design based on the original by
Andrew McKinley.

This happy breed of men, this little world,
This precious stone set in the silver sea.

King Richard II., Act II. i.

INTRODUCTORY.

SITUATION.—Lat. 54 degrees, 36 mins. (North), and Long. 9 degrees 15 mins. (West). The nearest point of the island from the mainland (Fair Head) is about three miles. The distance from the quay at Ballycastle to the landing place at Church Bay is seven and a half miles. The island is five and a half English miles long from the Bull, or western point, to Bruce's Castle on the extreme east, and upwards of four miles from Rue Point (the most southerly) to Altacarry Bay at the north-eastern extremity. The greatest breadth at any part is one and a quarter miles and the narrowest, half a mile. The highest point is 447 feet above sea level. The cliffs on the northern and western sides are extremely precipitous; the average elevation of the island is about 200 feet.

AREA.—3,500 acres (including Ushet Lough, 30 acres, and other smaller loughs). Since 1722 it has constituted a separate parish, containing twenty-two townlands:

Roonivoolin.	Ballyconagan.
Carravindoon	Ballynagard.
Carravinally.	Kilpatrick
Kinkeel.	Knockans
Craigmacagan.	Ballygill North
Demesne.	Ballygill Middle
Ballynoe.	Ballygill South
Glebe.	Gleggan
Ballycarry	Kinramer North.
Mullindress.	Kinramer South.
Church Quarter.	Kebble.

POPULATION.—At present less than 200; probably about 190. Of these, 25 are members of the Church of Ireland (including six children); the remainder are

Roman Catholics. A century ago the population was over 1,000; in 1784 it is stated to have been 1,200, but this may be a slight exaggeration.

OCCUPATIONS.—(*a*) Agriculture. Much of the surface consists of rough grazing. There are from 70 to 100 acres now under cultivation. Farming is the chief occupation. Beans are the chief money-crop.

The First Appendix to the *Seventh Report of the Royal Commission on Congestion in Ireland* (1907) contains some interesting references to agriculture as it was then practised. "Over nearly the whole island," said the late Mr. John Byrne (Lloyd's agent in Ballycastle), in the course of evidence, "the land is held in rundale. In some cases one partner holds the inside grazing one year, and another partner has it the next." (By rundale is meant the division of the land into good, middling and bad ground, each tenant taking a share of these divisions, commonly called a rundale. Grazing was denominated by the term "sum." A sum consisted of either eight wethers, six ewes and six lambs, or a cow; a horse was regarded as one sum and a half). "In one or two townlands one ridge belongs to one man and the next one to another …One of the first steps that should be taken to improve the place should be the re-adjustment of the boundaries, leaving every man a farm to himself … As very little hay and only a small quantity of oats are grown, the fodder for cattle and horses during the winter is very scarce … During the summer they have to be herded on the hillocks and knolls among the cultivated plots during the day and kept in walled-in enclosures, locally known as 'fanks,' at night."

Remarkable advances have been made in

agriculture in recent years, and in one or two cases it is at least as progressive as farms of similar size on the mainland. One farmer has about eighty head of cattle. Young calves are purchased on the mainland, taken to the island and pastured until two years old. The word *Rathlin* has been translated *Ram's Island*, from which it may be surmised that it was so named from the richness of its pastures. About 500 Rathlin cattle are sold at the grading centre in Ballycastle each year; most of these have been pastured entirely in the open. There is now a farm tractor and threshing mill (worked by the tractor) on the island. This has proved an inestimable boon. These modern agricultural implements belong to Mr. Tony M'Cuaig, one of the most extensive farmers on the island. There are also two small motor cars. The land is now being bought out under the Northern Ireland Land Purchase Act. One and a half centuries ago the annual rent of the island, which was payable to the Gage family, amounted to £600.

OCCUPATIONS—*(b)* Industries. Kelp was formerly made in great quantities; the chief markets were Campbeltown and Glasgow. It was manufactured according to the following process: Several women assembled early in the morning. They collected the sea-weed recently washed on the shore by the tide, or cut it from the rocks round which it grows, when the absence of the tide admitted of their wading out so far. The sea-weed or wrack thus collected was spread along the shore, and when sufficiently dried by the sun, was put into a kiln. This was a rude elliptical structure, formed of sods and stones, about three feet in depth and open at the top. The weed was then set alight. From the strong heat produced, it incorporated into a glutinous matter and was gently stirred with a stick. In this state it was suffered to remain until it cooled and became hard. It was then called kelp. There was also some spinning of flax for market and of wool for home use. The present Manor House occupies the site of a range of weavers' cottages.

TIDES.—They run at nine knots during the springs and six knots at the neaps. The first of the ebb in Rathlin Sound runs into Church Bay in its strength for two hours, when it slackens for an hour. The flood then flows into the bay and runs there for nine hours, during which time the ebb runs along shore on the east side of the island; thus the flood on that side continues only three hours. On the north side the tides are an hour later than on the south side.

AMPHIBIA. Common seal (Phoca Vitulina). In former times its skin and oil were much prized, the skin for making shoes, caps, etc., and the oil for burning. Frogs are not found on the island.

BIRDS.—Over 130 species of land and sea birds are included in *The Birds of Rathlin Island, Co. Antrim,* by Robert Patterson, M.B.O.U. "The Kinramer or western end," says Hamilton, "is craggy and mountainous. . . . A single native is here known to fix his rope to a stake driven into the summit of a precipice, and from thence, alone and unassisted, to swing down the face of the rock in quest of the nests of sea fowl."[1]

---

[1] *Letters on the Coast of Antrim,* p. 19.

EARLY HISTORY.

The island is one that flings its roots far back into the historic past. It has a human history extending over some thousands of years. Flint is abundant, and evidence goes to prove that a flourishing Neolithic industry existed on the island. "This industry," says Mr. T.H. Mason, "on account of its magnitude, was evidently of an export nature; in fact, the island and the adjoining coast of County Antrim would appear to have held in the late Stone Age the position that Detroit holds at present in the motor age.[1]

Rathlin is mentioned by Pliny as "an island between Ireland and Britain," while the celebrated Egyptian mathematician, astronomer, and geographer, Ptolemy, who lived in the second century A.D. and who wrote a description of the various countries of Europe, illustrated with maps prepared under his direction, also refers to it in his geography. Ptolemy was a noted geographer; he maintained that the earth was a fixed body in the centre of the universe, the sun and moon revolving round it. In addition to his reference to Rathlin, Ptolemy also mentions two rivers in the northern part of Ireland, which are believed to be those now known as the Foyle and the Bann. It is a truly remarkable fact that the island was known to Ptolemy and Pliny, celebrated Greek and Latin authors respectively, just as it possesses an interesting contact with the "magician who found a means of transmitting signals from shore to shore and from ship to ship "—the world famous Marconi, perhaps the greatest genius of modern times, who carried out certain experiments on Rathlin almost fifty

---

[1] *Islands of Ireland, p. 7*

years ago.

The early history of the island is very largely unknown until the sixth century A.D. when about the year 580 the famous St. Comgall of Bangor landed on Rathlin and founded the first Christian church. This church or "cell" was, of course, of the type peculiar to the early Celtic Church, and was almost certainly built of wattles and clay. It seems unlikely to have been a Culdean foundation, but if it was, it consisted of a body or college of ecclesiastics who occupied an intermediate position between the monastic and parochial clergy. Whatever its character, its foundation is of unusual interest for at least two reasons. First, it was almost exactly contemporaneous with the arrival of St. Columba at Iona. Only seventeen years previously, in A.D. 563, Columba and his twelve disciples set sail in their frail coracle from "Foyle, his oak-crowned river" (as Mrs. Alexander expresses it) for Iona, where they landed on May 12th of that year (being the eve of the Feast of Pentecost or Whitsun). It is difficult to imagine how hazardous it must have been, journeying in those far-off days in the frail coracles then in use from the Western Ocean to the Nile ;—

> *"The bending willow into barks they twine,*
> *Then line the work with spoils of slaughtered kine;*
> *Such are the floats Venetian fishers know,*
> *Where in dull marshes stands the settling Po;*
> *On such, to neighbouring Gaul, allured by gain,*
> *The bolder Britons cross the swelling main."*

In A.D. 574—only six years before St. Comgall landed on Rathlin—St. Columba had crowned Aidan King of the Dalriadic Scots in Iona, the first recorded Coronation Service in these islands. Secondly, the present parish church occupies the situation of Comgall's foundation of almost fourteen centuries ago—surely a thought that in an outpost such as Rathlin, bids us stop and reflect upon the utter transience of our earthly lives! The ancient church was known by the name of *Teampoll Cooil* — "The Church of Cooal" (Comhghaill). Only two other parish churches in North Connor now occupy the site of the ancient ecclesiastical foundations of Celtic times — St. Patrick's, Coleraine, and St. Patrick's, Armoy. Thus from the days of Comgall of Bangor, product of a seminary from which it is said King Alfred the Great procured professors for the schools he had established in the Britain of his day, a Christian foundation has existed on the island. Thus across the centuries — fourteen of them — we can reach towards the pioneer of Christianity in this remote outpost.

It may at first appear strange that a spot so remote and insular as Rathlin should have been selected at so early a period, as the residence of men who could not have failed to find a wider and more ample field for their labours in the extension of Christianity, but, generally speaking, the more ancient these religious foundations are, the less they seem to be dedicated to worldly objects and the love, of ease and luxury. Pious seclusion and meditation were especially coveted in the choice of places for their establishment. Think of the utter   remoteness

Rathlin Island

Rathlin East Lighthouse.

of those remarkable Christian remains off the coast of Co. Kerry — Skellig Michael — an island which has been aptly described as "the most, western of Christ's fortresses in the ancient world." The history of those times shows us that the Gospel had been extensively preached throughout Ireland at that early period and that small, and apparently insignificant, islands such as Rathlin were often the favourite resorts of the first Christian teachers. Indeed, there is hardly one amongst the many islands of Ireland in which some traces may not still be found of the early introduction of the Christian faith. Besides all this, it. must be remembered that from the sixth to the ninth century, Ireland stood at the head of European culture. This Western Isle became a refuge of Christian culture and a home of peaceful progress, attracting to its shores many students from Britain and Western Europe.

The ancient church of Rathlin, being an appendage of the renowned Abbey of Bangor, was almost certainly dedicated under the invocation of St. Comgall.[1] According to the tradition of the islanders it was so dedicated. The rectorial tithes of the island belonged to the successors of St. Comgall in the Abbey of Bangor until its suppression in the reign of Henry VIII. At the time of the dissolution Bangor was occupied by a community of the third order of Saint Francis which had settled there in 1469. The church was maintained for a long series of years, until the violence and rapacity of the Northmen in 790 A.D. and on divers subsequent occasions completely annihilated its little religious community, destroyed the wattle church and drove out its pastors. Thus it is

---

[1] The Copeland Islands off the coast of County Down also belonged to the Abbey of Bangor.

that no trace has remained of its existence, except for the succession of its bishops and abbots, which is undoubtedly authentic and is a most interesting record of the piety and zeal of these primitive Christians. In the early Celtic Church the Abbot or Superior of the monastery was the great person materially, not the bishop. That is why the succession lists of Abbots are for the most part complete, while those of many of the Bishops are very sketchy. The Celtic Church was, in fact, ruled by the Abbots of the monasteries; the Bishops were reverenced for their piety, learning and ecclesiastical office rather than for any other claim they might possess of a more worldly nature. A bishop was normally attached to a monastery, but as a subordinate member of the monastic staff and not as its executive or spiritual head. He was superior to the Abbot only in his power of ordaining and discharging such ecclesiastical functions as are peculiar to a bishop. This subordination of the episcopate to the authority of the abbot, who was frequently a presbyter, if not actually a layman, constituted within the orbit of its influence, an insuperable barrier against the emergence of the diocese and diocesan or monarchical episcopacy, as we understand such to-day.

The end of the eighth century witnessed the first of a series of Danish or Norse descents on Rathlin. By the eleventh century all trace of a Christian foundation on the island disappears. The first place pillaged on the Irish coast was the island of Rechra, afterwards known as Lambay, off the coast of Dublin. The Scandinavians, or Norsemen, were the most skilful and daring sailors of the Middle Ages. "They were known," says Professor Trevelyan, "to avenge in the streets of Constantinople blood feuds begun among

themselves in Dublin."[1] For them the Atlantic—the
sea of darkness—had no terrors. Before the mariner's
compass had come into use in Europe they made
distant voyages in vessels often not so large as modern
pleasure yachts. Their only guides on those perilous
expeditions were the sun, the stars, and the flight of
birds.[2]

Rathlin is not included as such in the Taxation of
Pope Nicholas (1306-1307) because at that time it
formed part of what was then the very extensive parish
of Billy. Neither does it appear in the Terrier or
Ledger Book of Down and Connor, 1615. The
spiritual jurisdiction has always been enjoyed by the
Bishop of Connor, who received twenty shillings in
proxies out of the island, whereas all the islands which
lie off the west of Scotland are inside the jurisdiction
of the Bishops of the Isles, who never had jurisdiction
in Rathlin.[3]

---

1 *History of England*, p. 75.
[2] *The Student's American History*—D. H. Montgomery.
[3] **Proxies**. From early times, at the prescribed annual (or if the diocese
was of too great an extent, biennial, or at furthest, triennial) visitation of
the bishop to each church, it was a rule that he should be entertained by
the parish priest This entertainment was styled *procuratio*, and when the
archdeacons, in after times, came to discharge a part of the visitorial
duties, the right of procuration was extended to them. In later times
procurations became very oppressive and, to prevent further abuses, it
was decreed by the Third Latern Council, in 1179, that archbishops, in
their visitations, were not to exceed a retinue of 40 or 50 horses; bishops,
20 or 30; archdeacons, 5 or 7; and rural deans, 5 or 7. As soon as the
bishops ceased to hold their itinerant visitations, the word procuration or
proxy came to signify a pecuniary composition paid to the Ordinary in
lieu of the discontinued entertainment.—Reeves' "Ecclesiastical
Antiquities" pp. 98-100. In Ireland, it was anciently the custom for the
archdeacon to receive procurations as well as the bishop; thus in the
Taxation of such dioceses as Cashel, Ardagh, Kildare, Ardfert and
Annaghdown (now incorporated in Tuam) the *procuration archidiaconi*
form an item. At the Reformation, the rates of proxies in the sees of
Down and Connor and Dromore varied from twenty, to two, shillings. A

The late Primate D'Arcy related that when he held the see of Down (1911-1919) he once asked, jestingly, the Bishop of Argyll and the Isles (Dr. Kenneth Mackenzie) to take Rathlin under his jurisdiction, but the Scottish bishop declined the offer! Doctor D'Arcy (as he then was) once spent a night on the island, staying in some little rooms belonging to a hospitable dweller who received him with great kindness in such quarters as she was able to provide. "How well I recall," he wrote, "our ramble in the fading light along the bleak cliffs of the north side of the island to the lighthouse, where, as night fell, we watched the circling of sea birds flashing through the beam of the light!"

---

revival of the custom was contemplated by the 17th Irish Canon, which prescribes that "the bishop shall, in his own person, every third year, at least, in the time of his visitation, perform the duty of Confirmation, etc." On the Scriptural principle, "Nemo cogitur sine stipendiis militare," was founded the rule that the bishop should be entertained by the parish priest at each church; which entertainment was called *procuratio* from *procurare* to refresh, as in the verses:—

Laeti bene gstis corpora rebus
Procurate viri (Virgil, Aen. IX, 158).

Bishop Mant penned the following lines after a visit to Rathlin in 1835 ;—

> *Isle of the northern sea! which, like the moon,*
> *Bend'st crescent-shaped mid Erin's floods before*
> *The face abrupt and high of grey Benmore;*
> *Rathlin, I reckon it no trivial boon*
> *To have scaled thy pathless turf yon autumn noon,*
> *And heard, conflicting with the ocean's roar,*
> *The sea-birds' cries, thick clustering on thy shore,*
> *Kenramer's cliffs, or pillar'd crags of Doon.*
> *Nor boon less welcome is it, nor less sweet,*
> *To have seen how knit with social charity*
> *In thy lone nook domestic virtues meet,*
> *And hospitable zeal. And, therefore, thee*
> *With kindly verse commemorative I greet*
> *And bid farewell, sequester'd Raghery.*

The island parish was also visited by the late Right Rev. J. F. M'Neice, D.D., Bishop of Down, etc. (1934-42). A Service Book and Prayer Book for the reading desk each contains an inscription stating that they were "kindly and generously presented to Rathlin Parish Church by the Right Rev. Thomas James Welland, D.D., Lord Bishop of Down and Connor and Dromore, during the curacy in charge of the Rev. J. A. W. M. Kerr, B.A., April, 1901." It is of interest that the Rev. John Archibald William Montgomerie Kerr (who died in Rathlin in 1916 and is buried in the parish churchyard), was the grandson of the Rev. John Kerr, B.A., Rector of Termonfeckin, diocese of Armagh, who was the personal friend of the Rev. Henry F. Lyte, author of the hymn, "Abide with me.'[1] The Rev. John Kerr was sometime tutor to Archibald William Montgomerie, 13th Earl of Eglinton, twice

[1] Canon J. B. Leslie, *Armagh Clergy*, p. 420.

Lord Lieutenant of Ireland. Rathlin is also visited from time to time by the Roman Catholic Bishop of Down and Connor. The Most Rev. D. Mageean, D.D., present Bishop of Down and Connor, has visited the island. In no part of his extensive diocese is His Lordship received with greater devotion and enthusiasm.

MEDIAEVAL TIMES.

When John de Courcy arrived in Ulster in 1177, he made friends with the local chieftains in Dalriada (of which ancient territory Rathlin formed a part). De Courcy was regarded by these local chiefs as their overlord, because he exercised full authority over them. He was responsible for the erection of Kilsantel Castle, which is either the "mote and bailey "structure at Mill Loughan, beside the ford of Camus, on the river Bann, or Mountsandel, near Coleraine. De Courcy was driven out of his possessions in 1205 by Hugh de Lacy, who was rewarded by King John with the title of Earl of Ulster. In 1210 de Lacy himself was driven out by the king. He was deprived of his earldom and his lands; the lands were thereupon given to Allen FitzRoland, Earl of Galloway, maternal grandfather of John Balliol and brother of Thomas, Earl of Athol, builder of the castle of Coleraine on the site of what used to be the Clothworkers' Arms Hotel in, that town. In 1227 de Lacy returned to favour, with the result that his title and territories were restored to him. At that time the northern part of the present County Antrim (including Rathlin) and the present North-East Liberties of Coleraine formed part of the Anglo-Norman county of Coulrath, with what is now the town of Coleraine as an important administrative centre. It was also called Twescard (Tuskard) meaning "north" and was the most lucrative part of the Earldom of Ulster. [1]

---

[1] The Earldom of Ulster was subsequently vested in Henry VIII by 28 Henry VIII, chap. 3. It has been held by different members of the Royal Family, as descendants of Hugh de Lacy, and is at present held by H.R.H. the Duke of Gloucester, K.G.K.T., K.P., brother of H.M. the King.—Lawlor, Ulster: its Archaeology and Antiquities., p. 212.

In 1242 Rathlin became the property of John Bisset, who had been outlawed for the murder at Haddington of Patrick, Earl of Athol. Escaping to Ireland he settled in the Glynns or Glens as he had obtained that district and the island of Rathlin from Hugh deLacy, first Earl of Ulster. The Bissets, a family which, it has been said, was of Greek origin, held Rathlin until they forfeited it because of Hugh Bisset's part in aiding Robert Bruce in 1306.[1] Scott in his *Lord of the Isles* refers to the sheltering on Rathlin of the future hero of Bannockburn, who has so indelibly written his name on the pages of history;—

> *The rebellious Scottish crew,*
> *Who to Rath-Erin's shelter drew*
> *With Carrick's outlawed chief.*

Bruce is said to have taken up his abode on the island in the "rycht stalwart castell," the ruins of which still bear his name. The association of Rathlin with the Bruce has been disputed by some. It has been asserted that after his defeat at Methven in 1306 Bruce found safety and protection among the people of the Norse earldom of Orkney, that he spent the winter of that year in the Bishop's Palace in Kirkwall, that in the spring of 1307 he was passed in security by his Norse friends down the Western Isles, and that he may have landed in Rathlin while arrangements were made for his advance on the Ayrshire coast. Barbour's poem, *The Brus*, informs us in quaint and almost unintelligible language, that the patriotic king set sail from Dunavertie Castle on south-eastern Kintyre, with a

---

[1] Mary Queen of Scots was the descendant of Walter Fitzalan, eighth hereditary High Steward of Scotland, and Marjorie, daughter of Robert the Bruce. Their son (Robert II) inherited the Scottish throne and was the first of the Stewart dynasty.

numerous fleet of galleys, "towart Rauchryne." Thus
Bruce really came to Arran and Ayrshire from
Rathlin, *but it was not there that he had wintered.* At all
events the connection with Bruce of what is now no
more than a fragment of crumbling wall, six feet high
at its highest point and situated on the north-eastern
corner of the island, has become such a firmly
established tradition that any attempt to disprove it
would seem quite futile. The ruin is peculiarly
interesting from the fact that its mortar embodies some
cinders of sea coal. This coal bears a close resemblance
to that of the Ballycastle coalfield and thereby appears
clearly to prove that the use of sea coal in the North of
Ireland was of considerably earlier date than is
generally supposed. Some pieces of the cement of this
ruined castle may be seen in the Museum of Trinity
College, Dublin. There is a good commanding view
from the castle of the whole eastern end of the island,
of Kintyre, and of the Sound of Jura, between Jura and
Islay.

Among those who accompanied Bruce to Rathlin
was a certain Sir Robert Boyd, ancestor of the Earls of
Kilmarnock—a title that merged into the present
noble family of Earls of Erroll. By a strange
coincidence, the oldest decipherable tombstone in
Rathlin churchyard is dated 9th December, 1665, and
marks the grave of James, fourth son of Andrew Boyd,
M.A., Minister of Eaglesham, who was appointed
Bishop of Argyll on the 4th March, 1613. Bishop Boyd
was a son of Thomas, son of the fifth Lord Boyd.
Archdeacon Craven, in his *Diocese of Argyll and the Isles,*
quotes Scott's *Fasti* entry regarding the bishop. James,
described as "of Rachrie," was excommunicated in
1646 by the Synod of Argyll (Presbyterian) for joining
the Marquess of Montrose and "M'Donald Coll-

Kittoch" in their rebellion. "It was the pretence of the Presbyterians," writes the Rev. Malcolm M'Coll, "that their revolutionary junta was the legitimate government of Scotland and that forces operating under King Charles's commission were rebels. . . Rathlin holds the mortal remains of a loyal cavalier."

Although naturally belonging to Ireland from its proximity to the Irish coast, Rathlin was early claimed as a Scottish island. At the time of Bruce's visit, it belonged to the lordship or kingdom of the Isles (though, as already indicated, the *spiritual* jurisdiction was always held by the Bishops of Connor). It continued to form part of this lordship or kingdom until 1476, when it became a part of the possessions of the Macdonnells of Islay and Kintyre. Dean Monro in his *Description of the Western Isles* says :— "On the south-west frae the promontory of Kintyre, upon the coast of Ireland, be four myle to land, layes ane iyle callit Rachlaine, pertaining to Ireland, and possessit thir mony[1] yeirs by Clan Donald of Kintyre, four myle lang and twa myle braide, guid land, inhabit and manurit."

In 1319 Rathlin was granted by Edward II to Sir John of Athy, but at some later date it was restored to the Bissets. It remained Bisset property until the death of John M'Evin Bisset as the result of a quarrel with some of the neighbouring barons. John M'Evin Bisset, who was the fifth in descent from the John Bisset who had been outlawed in 1242, left one child, Margery. There is romance in the story of this family and not least in the recognition in Scotland by Margery Bisset of King Richard II, whom she is said to have met on his second visit to Ireland. 1399. This lady recognised the king, disguised as a poor traveller, although it was supposed that he had met his death by starvation in

Pontefract Castle, or as Shakespeare has it, by murder at the hands, of Sir Pierce of Exton ;—

> *Exton, thy, fierce hand*
> *Hath with the King's blood stained the King's own*
> *land. Mount, mount, my soul! thy seat is up on*
> *high,*
> *Whilst my gross flesh sinks downward here to die.*

—Richard II, Act v, Scene v.

Margery Bisset, who was the daughter and heiress of John M'Evin Bisset, by his wife Sawe, or Sabia, daughter of a certain Hugh O'Neill, married about 1399 John Mor Macdonnell or John of Isla, second son of John, Lord of the Isles and grandson of Robert II, King of Scotland. As is well known, the Macdonnells (afterwards Earls of Antrim), as a result of this marriage became possessed of Rathlin and the Glens—an area practically co-extensive with the ancient territory of Dalriada.

THE GAGE FAMILY.

In the reign of James I, when the history of modern Ulster really begins, the northern part of Antrim (the Route and the Glynns), including the coast from Larne to Coleraine, was granted by patent to Sir Randal M'Sorley Macdonnell, K.B., afterwards first Earl of Antrim. Sir Randal, who was Sorley Boy's eldest surviving son, was fortunate enough to desert the falling cause of O'Neill in good time and so, in the words of Bagwell, realised "that parchment and not steel would in future decide the fortunes of families." From this first (and chief) grant, dated 28th May, 1603, the castle of Dunluce was at first excepted, but it was afterwards thrown in with the rest, as were the fishery of the Bann and the island of Rathlin. In 1746 the island was sold by Alexander, fifth Earl of Antrim, a nobleman noted for his extravagant habits, to the Rev. John Gage, M.A., Prebendary of Aghadowey, in the diocese of Derry. It is said that Gage purchased it with his wife's fortune. Mrs. Gage was a daughter of the Rev. John Johnston, M.A., Rector of Clondevaddock, Co. Donegal. Thus the island became the property of the Gage family, which continued to possess it until the passing of the Northern Ireland Land Purchase Act about twenty years ago. The Rev. John Gage was a native of Coleraine, and was a son of the Rev. Robert Gage, M.A., sometime Chaplain to Queen Anne.

Mr. Robert Gage, M.A., J.P., proprietor of Rathlin, who died in 1891, and great grandson of the Rev. John Gage, was a man greatly beloved. The Rev. Francis Laverty, Parish Priest of Rathlin 1883-87, said of him — "He took an interest in the island. It was his interest to do so. He knew the people individually and was the head of the island. He provided proper cattle for the islanders and gave facilities in regard to building boats, etc. He had a lime-kiln and brought a cargo of coal every year to the island so that the poor people could go any time they wished and get a hundredweight of coal." Mr. Gage, who died unmarried, was succeeded in the proprietorship of Rathlin by his brother, Major-General Ezekiel Gage, who died in 1906.

Since the coming to Ireland of the Rev. Robert Gage, practically every generation of the family has served in the armed forces of the Crown. Captain Ezekiel Hugh Gage, M.C., of the Royal Horse Artillery, died in 1931 at the early age of 34 ; his cousin, John, died at Salonika in 1918, aged 31 ; his cousin, Lieutenant John Stewart Moore Gage, Royal Inniskilling Fusiliers, was killed in action at the ever-memorable battle of the Somme, 1st July, 1916 ; Captain Richard Stewart Gage, J.P., Royal Dublin Fusiliers, accidentally met his death in tragic circumstances on the island in 1909; Major General Ezekiel Gage, of the Madras Staff Corps had a distinguished career in India ; while an ancestor, Frederick Gage, R.N., sailed with Sir Thomas Troubridge, R.N., and died of yellow fever in Jamaica during the Napoleonic Wars, aged 15. Lieutenant Arol Alexander C. Gage, R.N., lost his life in the war just ended; and, by a singular coincidence, in Church Bay, within sight of the little church which contains many memorials to the Gage family, a buoy marks the wreck of H.M.S. "Drake," in which Lieutenant Arol Gage's father, the Rev. Alexander H. Gage, M.A., T.C.D. (since deceased) served for a time as Chaplain during the War of 1914-1919. The two sons of Mr. E. B. Gage, nephew of Rev. A. H. Gage, also served in the second World War. Major General R. F. O'Donnell Gage, C.B.E., M.C., Royal Engineers, served in the first, and second World Wars. In June, 1946, Her Majesty the Queen of the Netherlands conferred on him the honour of Knight Commander of the Most Excellent Order of Orange Nassau, with swords. He was twice mentioned in dispatches for gallant service in North Africa and in Italy. He is the younger son of the late Captain Richard Stewart Gage, and grandson of Major-General Ezekiel Gage. Major-General R. F. O'Donnell Gage is carrying on the tradition of one of Ireland's foremost military families. He is the representative of the main, or Rathlin Island branch of the Gage family and is sixth generation in direct male descent from the Rev. Robert Gage, Queen Anne's Chaplain. His cousin is Mr. E. B. Gage, of Coolnamara, County Westmeath.

In January, 1758, the Rev. John Gage presented a petition to the Irish Parliament in which he "humbly proposed a scheme to Parliament to render the collieries on the northern coast of Ireland more useful, the navigation in and out of St. George's Channel *(sic)* more, safe and other purposes for the advantage and safety of the Channel trade." The petition is as follows:

"SHEWETH:

"That the Island of Rathlin is opposite Ballycastle colliery, distant about one league, and from Islay and Kintyre eight leagues. In the Northern entrance into St. George's Channel the same wind that brings ships into the mouth of the Channel will not always bring them up the Channel, and for want of a resting-place several ships have been lost. There is good anchorage in the Church Bay and Arkill Bay, in ten to twenty fathom water, with still at bottom, where ships from three hundred tons and upwards, with strong tackle, may ride out any storm, but vessels are frequently lost for want of a sheltering-place.

"That in the inner angle of the Church Bay there is a natural harbour of forty perches broad, and sixty long, which would receive ships under three hundred tons, where they might ride safely in all storms, were a pier erected on the western shore, to break off the western surge, on a natural rock which runs out about twenty perches, most of it dry at low water; and another on the south-east, shore, on another natural rock, dry also at low water; this would save numbers of vessels sailing in and out of the Channel from perishing, and might be completed for two thousand pounds.

"That at the Ushet, in the south point of the island, is a small natural port, opposite to the colliery, distant one league, which, by enlarging and scooping, might be made capable of receiving a number of vessels of one hundred tons, and might be completely finished for three thousand pounds; and these two harbours and bays would answer all the purposes of a safe navigation in and out of St. George's Channel, and the Ballycastle colliery, or any other colliery, which has been, or may be hereafter, discovered on the northern coast, where there is no place so capable to be made a safe harbour from Lough Foyle to Lough Larne.

"That this is the only place where a port can be made to render the collieries of Ballycastle useful, or of advantage to the public, or proprietor, provided the proprietor of those collieries be obliged (for the large sums he has already received from the public) to employ a sufficient number of hands to work the said collieries and constantly keep a sufficient number of lighters and boats to load all vessels as they come in, without delay or partiality, and that under severe penalties, as well as that of full damages to the parties so delayed, either by want of coals or want of boats.

"That there were lately seven barrels of coal found on the face of a rock on the northern coast of Rathlin, and opposite to it is a free stone rock, where it is supposed the vein ends; if this should prove fact, the pit would open on the intended pier.

"That in the reign of Queen Anne, the Church Bay in this island was a lurking-place for French privateers, who, from the heights in the island, could discover all vessels coming in or going out of St. George's Channel, from Tory Island and the western islands of Scotland to the Mull of Galloway. A King's ship stationed here would not only protect the trade from French depredations, but also intercept all smugglers, who now in vast numbers carry on their illicit trade, to the prejudice of His Majesty's revenue and the fair trader, and where a fishing-boat cannot pass undiscovered, through a vast tract of sea and channel.

"That all the herrings that enter St. George's Channel must pass by this island; and there are numbers of herring-hogs or porpoises constantly tumbling in the bay and in the north of the island. Between it and Islay is a cod-bank, with plenty of red cod; were there convenient harbours in this island, these three fisheries might prove of great advantage to the general public.

"That this island is likewise a most convenient place to fix a public granary, where great stores of corn, in cheap seasons, might be brought from the islands and continent of Scotland, where rents are mostly paid in grain, and in scarce years might supply the northern parts of this kingdom at moderate prices.

"That were a lighthouse erected on this island, and another on the island of Tory, vessels coming from the north or west seas would not lose sight of some one lighthouse[1], from the north-west point of Ireland to Howth Head, as there is already erected a lighthouse on the Copeland Island.

"That this, with a port at Ballintoy, for the reception of small craft, is humbly proposed as most necessary to render the collieries on the northern coast of Ireland more useful, the navigation in and out of St. George's Channel more safe; and other purposes for the advantage and safety of the channel trade.

---

[1] "some one lighthouse", as appears in. the original. Clachan editor.

"The Island of Rathlin is five miles long and one broad (Irish measure), contains about two thousand plantation acres, one hundred and thirty families, is a distinct parish, with a church and parsonage house."

To the above petition the Rev. John Gage appended the request that, as he was then old and infirm—he was sixty-five years of age—and unable to superintend the works, the money, if granted, should not be placed at his disposal. He was anxious not to be held responsible for its outlay, and, at the same time, that the Government should exercise the strictest supervision in the matter. His proposal, however, does not seem to have found favour with the authorities, as we do not meet with any traces of it afterwards in the House of Commons.

About the middle of the eighteenth century annual grants were made by the Irish Parliament for promoting harbour works, inland navigation, tillage and many other schemes connected with trade and industry. In 1755 there was a surplus of money in the Irish Exchequer of nearly half-a-million pounds sterling. As soon as this fact became known, petitions from almost every county in Ireland poured into the Irish House of Commons, asking for grants in aid of proposed improvements to lands, harbours, drainage, navigation and such like projects, as various as the interests and machinations of the petitioners. Those who possessed political influence and were not bound to vote in Parliament as the mere tools of patrons, by whose nominations they held their seats, generally succeeded in obtaining a share of the money granted for public and quasi-public purposes to carry out schemes of improvement on their estates, or on the estates of their relatives.

This document was accompanied by a curious little map of Rathlin which seems to have been pretty accurately prepared. The distance from the island to several surrounding points are exhibited, whilst the celebrated cod bank is given—perhaps in more than its due proportion on the scale. Islay and Kintyre are distant from the northern and north-eastern coasts of the island eight leagues respectively, Ballintoy two and a half leagues, and the collieries near Fair Head, only one league. The tide at the Bull Point is stated to be "strong at ebb." and Slough-na-morra ("the hollow of the sea") is described as "strong" both at ebb and flow.

Unfortunately O'Laverty in his *Diocese of Down and Connor*, vol. iv., p. 372, identifies *Coire-Brecain* or Brecan's cauldron with *Slough-na-morra. Coire-Brecain* is *outside* Rathlin—i.e., between the island and the Scottish islands, whereas *Slough-na-morra* is between Rathlin and the Irish mainland-—i.e., in Rathlin Sound, between Rue Point and Ballycastle strand.[1] Adamnan in his *Life of St. Columba* occasionally alludes, to Coire-Brecain. He relates that when Columba was conveying the remains of St. Kieran of Clonmacnoise to Iona, the ship was driven by a tempest "into a certain charybdis, which is named *Coire Brecain*, a most

---

[1] Slough-na-morra is roughly 3 or 4 miles off Ballycastle. At Slough-na-morra there is what is called on naval charts an "overfall"—i.e., an area where the sea breaks heavily with certain- tides and winds. When the ebb tide is flowing westwards, the first branch of it, or as the fishermen call it, the West Bush of the ebb, passes near Rue Point and pushes its way down the channel. The word "Bush" means a river in flood or in spate. The flood tide on the Ballycastle side is still flowing eastwards towards Fair Head, and the ebb tide, pushing its way through on the Ballycastle side, meets the flood tide. Where the tides meet, there is this "overfall" or turmoil. It is said that the ebb tide goes underneath the oncoming flood tide. There have been some fatal boating accidents in Slough-na-morra. It resembles somewhat the "Merry men of Mey" off the north coast of Scotland, between the mainland and Orkney.

dangerous whirlpool of the sea, in which, if a ship enters, it escapes not." The Coire-Brecain mentioned by Adamnan is far out in the North Channel. There does not appear to be any connection, as has been too readily assumed, between *Brecain* and Bracken's cave on the eastern side of the island.

Cox in his *History of Ireland*, vol. i., p. 73, states that in the reign of Edward I, 1274, "the islanders and Scots made an incursion into Ireland, burning several towns and villages, killing everyone they could get, and carrying off vast booty. Soon afterwards Sir Richard de Burgo and Sir Eustace Le Poer entered the island and burnt the cottages, slew all they met and smoked out those that hid themselves in caves, after the manner of smoking a fox out of his earth." At the dissolution of the religious houses, the rectorial, or large, tithes of Rathlin were appropriate to William O'Dornan, last abbot of the Abbey of Bangor. It will thus be observed that the ecclesiastical connection between the island and St. Comgall's famous monastic foundation at Bangor extended for almost a thousand years. "The whole seaboard of North Antrim," writes Doctor D. A. Chart, "abounds with old forts and castles; naturally so, for it was a coast exposed to hostile landings from the opposite Scottish shore. There are also a number of ruined churches, usually of that simple type which indicates an existence of not less than eight or nine hundred years.[1]

[1] History of Northern Ireland, *p. 89.*

A QUESTION OF LANGUAGE.

After the dissolution of the monasteries, the rectorial tithes were granted to Rice Aphugh, subsequently to John Thomas Hibbots, and in 1605 to Sir James Hamilton, first Lord Claneboye, a hard and unscrupulous Scotsman, who had become a Fellow of Trinity College, Dublin, on its establishment and had acted as an agent for James VI and I. In the reign of Queen Elizabeth the island is described as "very barren, full of heath and rocks, and there are no woods at all in it"—a description that pretty well corresponds to its present topography, except that more land is now under cultivation. It was in this reign that Rathlin was the scene of a very horrible massacre of the Macdonnells, perpetrated by the Earl of Essex at the instigation of the English government. The great Francis Drake was in Carrickfergus in 1575 and, in conjunction with Captain John Norris, undertook an expedition against the Scottish Macdonnells in Rathlin. Froude in his *History of England* refers at some length to this atrocity, which was hardly less appalling, though much less known, than the memorable Massacre of Glencoe in 1689.

The *Ulster Visitation Book*, 1622, states; "Grange de Rawdines; the second part of all tithes impropriate to the Abbey of Bangor and possessed by the Earl of Antrim. No vicar nor curate, it being not able to maintain one, neither can the people come to be served elsewhere, it being remote, and an island in the sea." Though Rathlin had been leased to trustees in 1637 by the Earl of Antrim, to assist in paying debts on his estate, it was declared to be forfeited by the Cromwellians for the part Lord Antrim took in the wars of 1641. These wars found Rathlin confiscated, with the Earl of Argyll appointed as governor. He had been sent with a regiment to assist in quelling the terrible rebellion that had broken out in Ireland in that year, when, in the words of Lord Macaulay, "a universal massacre ensued; nor age, nor sex, nor infancy were spared; all conditions were involved in the general ruin."

The Scots literally swept Rathlin bare of every living thing, hurling even the women over the cliffs. This desperate struggle took place at Lag-na-vista-vor, "the hollow of the great defeat, "and the hill above it is called "the hill of screaming." It was a stern persecuting age, near the close of the Thirty Years' War on the continent, and it is only too probable that the Scots would regard the slaughter of the unhappy Roman Catholic inhabitants as a sacrifice of righteousness and alike to the extermination of the Canaanites. Thus we find that many dark deeds were committed on the inhabitants of this lonely neighbourhood in former times.[1] The chaplain in Argyll's regiment — now represented by the Scots Guards — was the Rev. John Baird, M.A. (Glas.) to whom it fell to preach the sermon at Carrickfergus on the 10th of June, 1642, on the occasion of the constitution of the first Irish Presbytery of the Presbyterian Church—sometimes called the Army Presbytery.

The Down Survey records ;—

"The Parish or Island of Rathlin lyeth between the Dewcallidonian and Irish Sea, whose figure is represented by an Irish stocking, the toe whereof pointeth towards the Maine land. . . . This island by

---

1 *Massacres were committed on the island in 1558 (Sidney); 1575 (Essex) and 1642 (the Campbells).*

reason of the affinite with Scotland is inhabited with Scots, who, in former times (as is reported) contended with the Irish for this island, claiming it by the shallower sea between them and it, but upon tryall by some seamen to whome it was referred, they found upon a ridge of sand running between Point Fairhead and the Bay of this island, the sea was shallowest, therefore awarded it to Ireland." There is actually documentary evidence extant in the form of State Papers which indicates that it was decreed on a certain occasion in all seriousness and solemnity that Rathlin belonged to Ireland, rather than to Scotland. This was because no snakes were found within its borders—these having been previously banished by St. Patrick, thus turning the scales in favour of the inclusion of the island as part of Ireland!

The shrewd and wily Lord Deputy, Sir Arthur Chichester, by way of reply to the Scottish claim to the island, declared that "If it be of Scotland, we who have served the crown, have runne into greate errore, for in tyme of the rebellion, we often wasted it, and destroyed the inhabitants by the sworde, and by the halter, as we did the rebels of Ireland; soe did Sir John Perrott in the tyme of his government, of which noe complainte was made by anie subject of Scotland."

The island was restored to the Antrim family soon after the restoration of the monarchy in 1660 and continued in the possession of the Earls of Antrim until its sale to the Gage family in 1746, reserving the royalties and a rent of £100 per annum. The Gage family purchased the royalties in 1813. Hamilton in his *Letters on the Coast of Antrim,* written in 1784, says; "A good many years ago Lord Antrim gave orders to his huntsman to transport a couple of foxes into the island, for[1] the purpose of propagating that precious breed of animals. But the inhabitants assembled in consternation, and having subscribed each a hank of yarn, prevailed on the huntsman to disobey orders. However, he was sharp enough to take the hint and for some years paid his annual visit to Raghery, for the purpose of raising a regular tribute, to save the poor islanders from those desolating invaders." *The State of the Diocese of Connor*, 20th February, 1693, contains the following under Agherton (Portstewart), formerly the corps of the Treasurership of Connor; "The Treasurer, Mr. Thomas Jones, is chaplain to the Bishop (Doctor Samuel Foley), where he stays for the most part and has employed one, Mr. M'Gamell to serve the cure; not qualified for that place, but might be provided for in the island of Rathlin, because he can preach in Irish, where a great many Irish Protestants live and are apostatized for want of service. . . . " In the reign of Queen Anne (1702-1714) a French privateer found a permanent station in Church Bay to the great annoyance of trade.

The island was originally part of the parish of Billy. By the Charter of Connor, 1609, its rectorial and vicarial tithes went to form the Billy portion of the Archdeacon's corps in the chapter of the diocese. Some time before 1700—probably during the episcopate of the illustrious Jeremy Taylor (1661-67)—Rathlin became part of the parish of Ballintoy which had been separated from Billy towards the end of the seventeenth century. Its connection with Ballintoy was destined to be of short duration as an Act of Council dated April 20th, 1722, declared it an independent parochial unit. From 1722 until the Disestablishment it was a separate rectory in the gift of the Bishop of the diocese. In 1721 a pamphlet entitled the *State of the Case of the Island of Rathlin* was published, a few months after his consecration, by Dr. Francis Hutchinson, Lord Bishop of Down and Connor. Although mainly an appeal for funds to build a church, which was the immediate predecessor of the present building, the pamphlet is in many ways a most interesting document. The bishop relates that "Rathlin is an island in a deep and rough sea, two leagues from the County of Antrim. . . . . It is about five miles long and one broad and hath in it, as appears by a late exact computation, about 490 souls, who speak Irish with very little English mixt. It belongs to the parish of Ballintoy, in the diocese of Connor, of which parish the Rev. Dr. Archibald Stewart is rector, but the distance, tempestuousness of the sea and their ignorance of the English tongue, makes that they receive very little benefit from his best endeavours." Apparently Doctor Stewart, or his curate, merely crossed occasionally and held a service. The Communion plate, presented by a Mr. Charles M'Neale, is dated 1719, and so is actually older than the church, erected in 1722 through the efforts of Bishop Hutchinson. This is very likely explained by the circumstance that for some years before the erection of the church, occasional services were held on the island in some private dwelling. Such a state of affairs was by no means uncommon in the Established Church in Ireland in the eighteenth century. As there was then neither Manor House nor coastguard station, Divine Service may have been performed in the large slated building in the townland of Ballynoe.

Portion of the Communion plate of Ballycastle Church dates from 1738, as hall-marks clearly indicate. It is inscribed "Ballycastle Church," yet the building was not erected until 1756. (Ballycastle Church, upon its erection by Colonel Hugh Boyd, was a private chapelry and is not to be confused with the *parish* church there, known as Ramoan; both are still used for public worship).

It was the Most Rev. the Lord Primate of All Ireland (Thomas Lindsay), who was a great benefactor of the Church of Ireland, the Bishop of the Diocese, the minister and people of Ballintoy, and the inhabitants of the island that desired Rathlin to be created a separate parish, "and have a church as there hath been in ancient times, a resident minister, a parsonage house, etc." The reference to "ancient times" is undoubtedly to the church and religious community that existed on the island in the sixth century. The ancient *Teampoll cooil* or Church of Comghaill remained in ruins until 1722 when the predecessor of the existing church was erected.

The Bishop held the islanders in the highest esteem. He laments that there is no "school for the instruction of their children though they are very well disposed towards religion and very capable of civil improvements." To remedy this state of affairs he advocated the setting up of "a very good English free school in which, without Latin, the master shall be able to improve them in writing, arithmetic and all such knowledge as may fit them for trade and navigation." It is significant that the manager of this new school is to be "the officer of the King's customs for the time being" and not the incumbent of the parish. Apparently the bishop had some qualms about the wisdom of appointing clerical managers !

Two problems of great importance confronted the Bishop in his efforts to provide a church and school for the islanders. The first was the question of the language. Indeed Doctor Hutchinson refers to this as "our greatest obstruction." How could "the means of religion and learning (be applied) to them in English," because Irish was their mother tongue? The Bishop hoped to get over the difficulty in the following manner; "By the common method of teaching French and other languages, it is seen by experience that the easiest way of learning a new language is by having the known tongue and the tongue to be taught in two columns placed over against one another, so as one may be like a construing book to the other." "We hope," he continues, "to procure primers, catechisms, and, if it may be, psalters, common prayer books, Testaments, etc., with such double columns. And as this island is as yet under no pre-possession from the faults of the English alphabet, we propose to spell both languages by an alphabet formed, as near as may be, by the most perfect rules. As by this means we hope the children will learn English in half the time it is now taught in our common schools, where nothing but long practice can fix in their memories the different sounds of the same letters and diphthongs, so we hope we shall advance them so much the further in knowledge that is really useful." Whether this method of giving instruction in—what was to the islanders—a modern foreign language, would meet with the approval of our present day educationalists, is a matter which does not concern us here. One would like to know what success attended Doctor Hutchinson's efforts in this connection.

The second problem—no less important than the first—was the provision of an income for the maintenance of the minister, who would reside on the island when the new church was erected. This difficulty was overcome when the Right Honourable the Commissioners of First Fruits directed the Bishop and minister of Ballintoy to treat with the impropriator[1] for buying in the great (or rectorial) tithes to be added to the small (or vicarial) tithes, which Dr. Stewart, Rector of Ballintoy, was willing to separate from that parish and appropriate to the future incumbents of Rathlin. A certain Colonel and Mrs. Corry were not only so kind as to part with the great tithes at a reasonable rate for the sake of promoting the good work, but out of further piety promised twenty pounds out of the purchase money towards laying the foundation of the church. It is not clear in what circumstances Corry became possessed of the rectorial tithes.

Bishop Hutchinson notes the extreme importance of the position of Rathlin. "As this island," he says, "lies in a great road for ships passing from Norway, Denmark, Scotland, the northern parts of America, Coleraine and Derry ... we shall be glad to add any conveniences for strangers who shall be driven in thither by distress of weather." The motive underlying such a reference is obvious! Doctor Hutchinson was also particularly anxious that the islanders should possess a library. "Already," he notes, "we have subscriptions for a good number of books for a settled library, to be fixed either in some part of the church, or in a room in the parsonage house, for the use of succeeding ministers, schoolmasters, or strangers." The bishop purchased a collection of books for the islanders, partly at his own expense, and partly at that of Archbishop William King, among the most distinguished of the occupants of the see of Dublin, and of Charles, second Duke of Grafton, K.G., grandson of the Merry Monarch.

The bishop was also responsible for publishing a

---

[1] a person to whom a benefice is granted as their property, Clachan ed.

catechism in the Irish language. This was not the Church Catechism, as is generally supposed, but another catechism, probably compiled specially for Rathlin by the bishop himself. A copy of this interesting work, which has ever since been known as the *Raghery Catechism*, is in the possession of the Rev. Dermot M. Carmody, B.A., Nenagh, Co. Tipperary, son of the late Very Rev. W. P. Carmody, M.A., V.P.R.I.A., Dean of Down. The Gaelic dialect of the islanders was similar to that spoken in Kintyre and the Western Highlands of Scotland. Gaelic was almost universally spoken just over a century ago.

Bishop Hutchinson's church was dedicated under the invocation of St. Thomas, no doubt because the Christian name of the Lord Primate of All Ireland at that time (Archbishop Lindsay) was Thomas. His Grace had taken a practical interest in the efforts to provide a church and in those days it was sometimes deemed more fitting thus to associate the dedication than to use the name of the founder of the original church—St. Comgall—a truly amazing state of affairs! The Celtic Church was supported by land and offerings. Such land belonged to the saint and was considered his property. This was the origin of dedication in the early Church of Ireland. Churches were not dedicated to *dead* saints, but given to *living* saints and considered their property both in life and in death.

LATER HISTORY.

The first rector of the parish was the Rev. John Martin, previously curate of Ballintoy. He is probably the John Martin who, at the Triennial Visitation of 1694, is returned as serving the cure of Agherton (Portstewart) for the rector, the Treasurer of Connor. Martin held the parish until his death in 1740 at the age of eighty and is commemorated by a typically eighteenth century mural monument on the interior south wall of the church. A tablet in the German language is erected on the opposite wall to the memory of Carl Piehl by his brothers and sisters in Berlin and New Strelitz. Piehl died on the island on the 24th September, 1868, and is buried in the churchyard, where a headstone marks his grave. He was the faithful servant of a German prince, His Serene Highness Prince Albrecht of Waldeck and Pyrmont, who married (in the Chapel Royal, Dublin Castle, on 2nd June, 1864) Dorothea Gage, great aunt of Major General R. F. O'Donnell Gage. The title of Countess von Rhoden was given Miss Gage by the reigning Prince of Waldeck and Pyrmont after her marriage and descended to her sons and daughters.

One of the daughters married at Ramoan Parish Church, Ballycastle, on 2nd March, 1895, Mr. R. St. George Johnston, for many years sub-agent to Lord O'Neill at Shane's Castle, Randalstown, Co. Antrim. The Rev. Samuel Shone, B.A., T.C.D., afterwards (1884-1897) Bishop of Kilmore, Elphin and Ardagh, began his clerical career in Rathlin, having ordained for the curacy of the island parish in 1843.

Church of the Immaculate Conception.

In 1772 half the population was Protestant and the other half Roman Catholic. The condition of the people had been much improved by having a clergyman residing among them and the opportunity afforded them of becoming acquainted with the English language. In 1812, out of a population of 1,100 the number of Protestants was reduced to fifty. This was due to the carelessness of the Rev. James Moore, a rather unsatisfactory incumbent who held the parish for over half a century. It was as a consequence of the neglect of this incumbent that the library provided by Bishop Hutchinson, the Duke of Grafton, Archbishop King and others, was dispersed and lost.

The manufacture of kelp is said to have begun about 1774. In 1784, about one hundred tons of kelp were exported from Rathlin. It was purchased by the linen bleachers of the North of Ireland at £5 5s per ton, the whole amounting to more than £525. At that time, in a fruitful year, barley was exported to the value of £600. In 1775 the island became subject to its share of the Grand Jury assessments as part of the Barony of Carey. About ten years afterwards the road which runs from Ushet to Kebble—i.e., from one end of the island to the other—was begun and for many years there was no other. The Kebble or extreme western end is now almost, if not entirely, devoted to grazing. Apart from the lighthouse men at Rathlin West light, no one lives there now. In former days about seven families lived in comparative comfort in Kebble. The sward in parts is as green as a lawn, although it has not been cultivated for many years. Formerly distinctions existed between the inhabitants of each end of the island and the characteristics of

Ushet and Kenramer men were looked upon as totally
dissimilar. In 1820 a certain John Alexander
M'Donnell, who is described as "of Rathlin," died,
aged 60 years. He was the son of John M'Donnell of
Kilmore, Glenariffe, Co. Antrim, and was thus
connected with the Earls of Antrim. He is buried in
Layde old churchyard, near Cushendall, Macdonnell
was possessed of the head rent; of the island for a time.
This rent was payable by the Gage family.

The present church was completed about 1815 by
a grant from the Board of First Fruits, as the building
erected through the efforts of Bishop Hutchinson had
been rather poorly constructed and was so dilapidated
that a new church had become absolutely necessary.
It is said that the eastern part of the church is a portion
of the old building. It had been in a ruinous state for
some years before 1811—the year in which Mr.
(afterwards the Rev.) Robert Gage, M.A., J.P.,
attained his majority. "This gentleman is completely
lord of the isle and banishes his subjects to the
continent of Ireland for misconduct, or repeated
offences against the laws."[1] His father, also named
Robert, who was High Sheriff of Co. Antrim in 1787,
had died in 1801, consequently there was a minority
for ten years. Very agreeable relations existed between
the Gage family and their tenants. Evictions were
unknown and rents were settled by mutual agreement
without the intervention of the law courts. "The
tedious processes of civil law," wrote Hamilton, "are
little known in Raghery, and indeed the affection
which the inhabitants bear to their landlord, whom
they always speak of by the endearing name of master,

---

[1] Parliamentary Gazetteer of Ireland (Rathlin). 1844-45, Part VIII, pp.
134,135.

together with their own simplicity of manners, renders the interference of the civil magistrates very unnecessary. The seizure of a cow or a horse for a few days, to bring the defaulter to a sense of duty, or a copious draught of salt water from the surrounding ocean, in criminal cases, forms the greater part of the sanctions and punishments of the island. If the offender be wicked beyond hope, banishment to Ireland is the *dernier* resort, and soon frees the community from this pestilential member."[1]

In 1821 an establishment of coastguards was placed on the island and the range of houses (still inhabited) and situated on the shore of Church Bay just immediately beside the landing place, was built for their accommodation. In 1841 the population was 1,010; by 1881 it had decreased by practically one-third, being 361, of whom 254 were Roman Catholics and 107 Protestants. Since 1881 it has decreased by almost one-half.

In 1849 the Ballast Board (now known as the Commissioners of Irish Lights) purchased a small portion of land on the north-eastern angle of the island, in the townland of Ballycarry, for the purpose of erecting a lighthouse. The first stone of this lighthouse, which adjoins the existing lighthouse, was laid by the Rev. Robert Gage in that year. During the first world war an automatic light was placed on Rue Point at the southern extremity of the Island, while another excellent lighthouse (exhibiting a red flash only) and fog horn were erected near Bull Point. This is a warning light to vessels as they approach from the west and it is officially known as Rathlin West Light.

By a curious coincidence it is in the wintry month

---

[1] *Letters on the Coast of Antrim*, p. 19.

of December that the festivals of dedication of both church and Roman Catholic chapel occur—the former, the 21st December (St. Thomas) and the latter the 8th December (Immaculate Conception of the Blessed Virgin Mary). In the polity of the Roman Catholic Church the island was originally held with the parishes of Ramoan and Armoy. The parish priest of Armoy visited it every five or six weeks. Its association with that parish ceased about 1778, after which the Roman Catholics agreed to subscribe a sum sufficient for the maintenance of a priest. Since then there has always been one resident. The present Roman Catholic chapel was dedicated on the 22nd August, 1865. It took the place of one that had existed from 1817 and that was originally an old deserted mill. Until some years ago, the island was an independent parochial unit, but is now served (by means of a resident curate) from the staff of the parish priest of Ramoan (Ballycastle). The parish priest of Ramoan (the Very Rev. Archibald M'Kinley, V.F.) was at one time parish priest of Rathlin, so that he enjoys the somewhat unusual distinction of having been parish priest of the same parish twice. Before, and for some time after, the Reformation, members of the Franciscan order were on Rathlin. Friar Dominick O'Brallaghan, or Bradley, who died in 1746, also held the office of parish priest of the island.

In 1766 there were no less than thirty-five families on the island bearing the surname M'Curdy, which is evidently a contraction for MacGillabrighde, "son of the servant of Brigid. "The name of Somerled MacGillabride - the great thane of Argyll, is often corrupted by Norse chroniclers into *Sowdry Maclllurdy*, which has been further altered to *M'Curdy*. Other Rathlin family names include, or have included, those of Anderson, Black (one family of which came from the west of Ireland), Currie, Glass, Heggarty, Hunter, M'Kay, M'Quilkin or Wilkinson, M'Kinley, M'Mullan, Smyth, Weir, and M'Couaig, or M'Cuaig. The word M'Couaig used to be translated on the mainland into *Fivey*, because the Irish word *Cuig* is *five*.

Visitors to the island should endeavour to visit the sweat house in the townland of Knockans just over one mile W.N.W. of the parish church. Sweat houses were chambers heated to produce profuse sweating for the cure of rheumatic pains or allied ailments and for the invigorating effect their use produced. The Rathlin sweat house is shaped like a bee-hive and is constructed of rough uncemented stones. It is 5 feet in internal diameter, narrowing upwards in a corbelled roof to a 2 feet aperture at a height of 4 feet 3 inches from the floor. The entrance is a low rectangular opening 1 ft. 9 ins. by 1 ft. 6 ins. high, by 2 ft. 6 ins. deep. Opposite the entrance inside is an earthen ledge or seat, occupying nearly half the area of the floor. It may be paved with small slabs under the loose earth.[1] The entrance is at ground level and it was through this aperture that the patient crept on hands and knees. The peat fire, having been previously removed, the patient remained inside until the whole human frame became moist with perspiration. The door or aperture was closed during this process. When the sweating was completed, the patient was removed and was either wrapped up in warm clothing or immersed in cold water! Women engaged in the kelp industry found that the smoke from the burning seaweed greatly darkened their complexions; in an island where cosmetics were then probably unknown they underwent sweat house

[1] *Preliminary Survey of Ancient Monuments (Northern Ireland), p. 1.*

treatment as a form of beauty culture!

No account of Rathlin would be complete without some reference, however brief, to the association of the island with the great inventor, Guglielmo Marconi, the master of wireless development (though not the discoverer of electric waves), whose mother was an Irish woman, the daughter of Mr. Andrew Jameson of Daphne Castle, County Wexford. In May, 1898, Marconi at the instance of Lloyds, installed his apparatus at Ballycastle and Rathlin Island. A short time before this Lord Kelvin had visited Marconi's stations in the Isle of Wight and Bournemouth. Lord Kelvin, who was a native of Belfast, insisted on paying for the messages he sent, in token of his belief in the commercial and other possibilities of wireless telegraphy. Concrete blocks or foundations beside Rathlin East Lighthouse still bear their silent witness to the early days of one of the greatest inventions mankind has known. Mr. John Cecil, a Rathlin farmer, who resides near the place of these early experiments, can recall his association with the twenty-four year old inventor and how he was employed by him to assist in the erection of poles and other equipment pertaining to the apparatus. It is surely of more than ordinary interest that a Rathlin islander had thus an intimate connection with one of the most supremely significant characters of our time. Three years later, when the first signal—the letter "S "in Morse (three dots)—was transmitted from Poldhu in Cornwall across the Atlantic to Signal Hill, St. John's, Newfoundland, on 12th December, 1901, Marconi (who was at St. John's) showed no excitement, but calmly handed over the earphones, first to Mr. George S. Kemp, who was assisting him, and who was a well known figure in Ballycastle at the time of Marconi's Rathlin experiments. The writer's father still recalls his meeting Mr. Kemp, with whom he was well acquainted. It is but stating the bare truth to say that for centuries to come and in "states unborn and accents yet unknown, "Marconi's remarkable wireless developments will be still broadening their influence upon the lives of men.

THE PRESENT DAY.

In the war that has just ended, the coastguard lookout on the northern cliffs of the island, commanded a view of virtually the whole of the northern approach to these islands through the North Channel. As a strategic position in the matter of sighting vessels, it was unrivalled anywhere else on the coast of Northern Ireland. It will be remembered that Mr. Churchill more than once referred to this open northern approach in the course of some of his momentous broadcasts during six of the most eventful years in the long history of the British people. Off the northern coast of this little and seemingly insignificant island, set at the entrance to the North Channel, passed the convoys that preserved our life-line and delivered us (in Mr. Churchill's words) from that "slavery and death" that might well have been ours had all of the northern Irish coast, been neutral in the great struggle!

Viewed from the mainland, the cliffs, partly composed in places of basalt, and partly of chalk, have earned for the island the comparison in Kingsley's *Westward Ho!* to a drowned magpie. Rathlin has a connection by motor boat four times weekly with Ballycastle (water and landing conditions permitting), with an almost daily service in the summer season. Although the means of communication are still somewhat primitive—the motor boats not being very large—they represent an improvement on the sailing vessels of former days. Hamilton in his *Letters on the Coast of Antrim* thus relates his experience when crossing from Ballycastle in July, 1784;— "The little skiff in which I navigated, was built of very slight materials, and did not seem to me well calculated to buffet these stormy seas. I observed that we had received a good deal of water into it; and on expressing my uneasiness that there was no visible means of throwing it out, one of the boatmen instantly took off his brogue, with which he soon cleared the vessel of water, and put it on his foot again without seeming to feel the slightest inconvenience from the wetness of it, leaving me quite at ease on the subject of pumping the vessel." The present harbour facilities, particularly at Ballycastle, leave much to be desired, although as long ago as 1899 the Antrim County Council formed a Piers and Harbours Committee to deal with the piers and harbours around the coast. It sometimes happens in winter that boats may make the crossing to within a few yards of the harbour at Ballycastle, only to find that they are unable to effect a landing and so must perforce return again to the island!

A young Rathlin islander, Thomas M'Cuaig, whose father (now deceased) is mentioned in Waugh's *Irish Sketches* as having been born at the time of the dedication of the Roman Catholic chapel in 1865, thus wrote of Life on Rathlin in the *Ballycastle High School Magazine*, 1945 ;—

"On Rathlin Island the wheel of life revolves with uneventful regularity. ... In years gone past the island was entirely self-supporting, growing its own food and spinning its own cloth. ... A familiar feature of the island landscape is the thatched cottages. These are usually white-washed and, with painted windows and doors, make a very pleasing sight ... Like the ocean which swells about its shores and the smoke which curls in tranquil solitude above its cottages, Rathlin lives its life in peace and plenty. Often, indeed, the words of the poet come back to my mind as the best description of it all:—

'Oh! the homes are small in Rathlin,
But the kitchen fire is bright;
The kettle sings, the griddle swings,
And the barley bread is light.

Sure with milk, eggs, butter from the farm,
And fresh fish from the sea,
'Tis happier than the table
Of the king himself to me!"

"The best way of benefiting the people of Rathlin," said the Right Hon. Sir John Colomb, K.C.M.G., in 1907, "is, that assuming the means are granted to some authority, that that authority should devote its efforts to organising the people to help themselves and to develop industries that are suitable to the island."

The islanders, who are a sturdy, good-natured and peace-loving community, untouched and untroubled by critical questions, regarded Ireland as a sort of foreign kingdom in bye-gone times when education, social progress and the general standard of living were not what they are to-day. It has been very truly said that one of the rarest things in Rathlin is "a Rathlin man's blood shed in anger. The islanders may talk as much as they like, but they never strike." "May Ireland be your hinder end" was once a common and heavy curse among the dwellers of this romantic and fascinating isle of the northern sea. Like most of the inhabited island communities around our coasts, the twentieth century has seen Rathlin become less and less the self-contained community it once was.

Not only has the motor car, the tractor, the wireless and even on at least one occasion the aeroplane, invaded it, but in common with dwellers in the largest cities, the inhabitants of Rathlin must now somehow understand the mysteries of ration books, identity cards, coupons, points, the hundred and one government "forms" and other departmental paraphernalia which constitute such a marked feature of the grandmotherly government of the present day. In spite of all this, however, the Rathlin islanders probably come nearer a truer appreciation of the eternal values than those of us who live closer to the hurry, bustle and complexity of this modern age.

> *Serene above the ever murmuring sea.*
> *Romantic Rathlin rears her regal head;*
> *The trembling waves uprising grand and free*
> *Chant forth her praises round her rocky bed.*

List of duties (in addition to the rent) collected or taken in kind and payable to the landlord, the Earl of Antrim, about 1720. The yearly rent at this time was £109 7s 0d, but the Antrim estates were then let on very moderate terms owing to the alleged mal-administration of the agent, Alexander Stewart, brother of the Rev. Archibald Stewart, D.D., Rector of Ballintoy, which then included Rathlin (1718-1722). In 1784, when Doctor Wm. Hamilton, M.R.I.A., visited the island, the annual rent paid to Mr. Robert Gage (died 1801), son of the Rev. John Gage, was £600.

BARONY OF CAREY.

ISLAND OF RATHLIN.

Townland of—
Kenramer (Kinramer)—24 pullets and 10 sheep.
Ballygial (Ballygill)—24 pullets and 10 sheep.
Killpatrick (Kilpatrick)—12 pullets and 5 sheep.
Ballynavargan (Ballynagard)—24 pullets and 3 sheep.
Ballycarey (Ballycarry)—12 pullets and 5 sheep.
Ballynoe—24 pullets and 10 sheep.
Kankiel (Kinkeel)—24 pullets and 8 wethers.
More to be paid by the Inhabitants of the Island yearly—19 sheep.

-See Hill, *The Stewarts of Ballintoy*.

THE ENCHANTED ISLE.

This well-known ballad was published anonymously by the Rev. Luke Aylmer Connolly, B.A., T.G.D., Chaplain of Ballycastle Church, 1810 -1826. Connolly had studied in Trinity College, Dublin, along with Thomas Moore, the great Irish poet. The words were suggested by the various and fantastic forms assumed by the clouds in northern latitudes. Their shadows, reflected by the ocean, are said to bear a strong resemblance to the *Fata Morgana* of Rhegio[1]. Connolly relates how he received a minute description of this extraordinary appearance from several persons who saw the beautiful phantom on different summer evenings, along the Giant's Causeway shore. Shadows resembling castles, ruins and tall spires, darted rapidly across the surface of the sea. These were instantly succeeded by appearances of trees, lengthened into considerable height. The shadows moved to the eastern part of the horizon and at sunset totally disappeared. An enchanted island, containing all the characteristics of an aquatic paradise was supposed to be seen floating along the Antrim coast. "It is supposed by the peasants," says Connolly, "that a sod from the Irish *terra firma*, thrown on this island, would give it stability, but though several fishing boats have gone out at different times, provided with this article, it has hitherto eluded their vigilance."—Shaw Mason, *Parochial Survey of Ireland*, Vol. II, pp. 515, 516. When the Rev. George Hill, sometime Librarian in Queen's College, Belfast, as a boy attended a Classical school in Ballycastle in 1824-25 he frequently saw Connolly, then in infirm health. Connolly died on the 30th January, 1832, and is buried in the old churchyard of Ramoan, but no stone marks his grave.

---

[1] A mirage visible above the sea horizon of a narrow distorting band of light. Clachan ed.

To Rathlin's Isle I chanced to sail
When summer breezes softly blew,
And there I heard so sweet a tale
That oft I wished it could be true.
They say at eve when rude winds sleep,
And hushed is every turbid swell,
A mermaid rises from the deep
And sweetly tunes her magic shell.

And while she plays, rock, dell and cave
In dying falls the sound retain,
As if some choral spirits gave
Their aid to swell her witching strain,
Then summoned by that dulcet note
Uprising to th' admiring view,
A fairy island seems to float
With tints of many a gorgeous hue.

And glittering fanes and lofty towers
All on this fairy isle are seen,
And waving trees and shady bowers
With more than mortal verdure green,
And as it moves the western sky
Glows with a thousand varying rays;
The calm sea tinged with each dye
Seems like a golden flood of blaze.

They also say if earth or stone
From verdant Erin's hallowed land
Were on this magic island thrown,
For ever fixed it there would stand.
But when for this some little boat
In silence ventures from the shore
The mermaid sinks—hushed is the note;
The fairy isle is seen no more.

Bibliography.

In addition to the authorities cited in the text, other books, articles, etc., dealing in whole or in part with Rathlin include;—

Archdall, M.—*Monasticon Hibernicum* (Rathlin p. 11).

Ewart, L.—Handbook of the United Dioceses of Down and Connor and Dromore (Rathlin pp. 103—105*).

Hill, G.—*The Macdonnells of Antrim.*

Holmer, N.—*The Irish Language on Rathlin Island* (pub. by the Royal Irish Academy, 1942).

Joyce, P. W.—*Irish Names of Places* (3 vols.)

Lewis, S.—*A Topographical Dictionary of Ireland,* Vol. II, pp. 501, 502. Parish of Rathlin.

Mant, R.—*History of the Church of Ireland, Vol II.*

Manuscript Memoirs of the First Ordnance Survey of Ireland (Parish of Rathlin), preserved in the Royal Irish Academy, Dublin.

Miskimin, Samuel—*Rathlin Tides.* Dublin Penny Journal, p. 321.

O'Laverty, J.—*Diocese of Down and Connor,* Vol. IV.— Parish of Rathlin, pp. 351—396.

Parliamentary Gazeteer of Ireland (1844-45), Part VIII.— Parish of Rathlin, pp. 134, 135.

Proceedings, Royal Irish Academy, XLII, No. 7, 1934 (C. Blake Whelan).

Proceedings, Belfast Natural History and Philosophical Society, 1922-23 (The People of Rachrai), pp. 4—7. (Michael A. MacConaill).

First Appendix to the Seventh Report of the Royal Commission on Congestion in Ireland (1907).

Proceedings, Belfast Natural History and Philosophical Society, 1933-34, pp. 107—111 (C. Blake Whelan). Beeves, W.— *Ecclesiastical Antiquities of Down and Connor and Dromore.*

Ulster Journal; of Archaeology—First series.

Vol. II—The Description and Present State of Ulster 1586, p. 155

Vol. V—The Bruces in Ireland, p. 5.

Vol. VIII—Sydney's Memoir of his Government in Ireland, p. 193; also Vol. V, p. 316.

Ulster Journal of Archaeology—Second Series.

Vols. VI and VII — The Stewarts of Ballintoy (Hill, G.)

Vol. XII—Some Rathlin Place Names (Duncan, J.) pp. 132—134.

Vol. XVII—Some Antiquities of Rathlin (Morris, H.), p. 39.

Ulster Journal of Archaeology—Third Series.

Vol. II, Part II—Bibliography of Periodical Literature relating to the Archaeology of Ulster, p. 288.

Vol. Ill, Part I—Conditions of Life in Prehistoric Ireland.

Vol. V—A Hoard of Coins from Rathlin Island, p. 66.

Vol. VIII, Parts I and II—Field Archaeology in the Ballycastle District (Prof. E. Estyn Evans).

Vestry Book, Rathlin Parish 1769-1795 (copy in Public Record Office, N.I.)

Young, Mrs. A. I.—*Three Hundred Years in Innishowen* (for History of the Gage family of Rathlin Island and genealogical table), pp. 280—288.

Birds on rocks at West Lighthouse

THE BIRDS OF RATHLIN ISLAND

COUNTY ANTRIM

By ROBERT PATTERSON, M.B.O.U.

(Re-printed from *The Irish Naturalist)* Vol. I, 1892.
For much of the following information I am indebted to the late owners of the island, Robert Gage, Esq. (died 1891), and Miss Gage (died 1892). My own notes, taken on the island, have been consulted, and, of course, Thompson's *Birds of Ireland.* Dr. J. D. Marshall's paper on the statistics and natural history of the island (*Proceedings Royal Irish Academy*, 1836) and Mr. A. G. More's *List of Irish Birds* have been referred to. I have also taken some information from the *Reports on the Migration of Birds* (1881-1887), and have to thank Mr. R. J. Ussher for drawing my attention to an article in the *Zoologist* for 1867, by Mr. Howard Saunders, describing a visit he paid to the island. I am aware that Mr. Gage published a list of the birds of Rathlin in the *Proceedings of the Dublin Natural History Society*, but I have not been able to refer to it.

The species that are known to breed in Rathlin are marked with an asterisk (*).

*Turdus viscivorus, L.—Mistle-Thrush. Resident all the year; it breeds regularly, generally in the bare fork of a tree.

*T. musicus, L.—Song-Thrush. Common; breeds in all the gardens, more numerous[1] about Church Bay than elsewhere.

Turdus iliacus, L.—Redwing. Frequent in winter.

T. pilaris, L.—Fieldfare. Not so common as last.

*T. merula, L.— Blackbird. Common in the gardens and hedges, where it breeds.

T. torquatus, L.—Ring-ouzel. The only specimen ever seen was shot, 18th April, 1883, by one of the light-keepers (Migration Report for 1883).

*Saxicola oenanthe, L.—Wheat-ear. Very common during the summer, generally breeds in crevices of rocks and walls; earliest date of arrival, March 8th. I found it extremely abundant in June.

*Pratincola rubicola, L.—Stonechat. Frequently seen; nests generally among the whins.

*Erlthacus rubecula, L.~Robin. Dr. Marshall states that the Robin is rare, while Mr. Gage characterises it as common in the gardens and low bushy places, where it breeds. In 1889 I observed several young Robins, but did not see a single adult during three days.

Sylvia cinerea, Bechst.—Whitethroat. A regular summer visitant to the gardens, but the nest has not yet been found. I have no doubt it breeds.

Regulus cristatus, Koch.—Golden-crested Wren. A constant spring visitor, being frequently taken at the light-house on migration; it never remains on the island.

Phylioscopus rufus, Bechst.-Chiffchaff. An occasional visitor to the gardens. One was taken on an apple tree in March, 1862. It has never been known to breed.

P. trochilus, L.—Willow-wren. Rarely seen; one was caught alive near the light-house, and another found in Mr. Gage's garden in April, 1867.

Acrocephalus phragmitis, Bechst.—Sedge-warbler. This was the only bird I was able to add to Mr. Gage's list. I saw and heard the bird at Alley Lough, 2nd June, 1889. In October, 1891, a second example was killed by a Kestrel, and brought to Miss Gage.

*Accentor moduiaris, L. Hedge-sparrow. Common in the hedges and whins where it breeds. An albino young bird was once found beside the nest.

Parus major, L.—Great-tit. An occasional visitor. One was taken in January, 1862, in Mr. Gage's garden, others have been seen at intervals.

P. coeruieus, L.—Blue-tit. Occasionally seen; one was found dead in the garden in 1891.

*Troglodytes parvulus, Koch—Wren. Very common and resident, generally builds in ivy. Often observed on migration.

Certhia familiaris, L.—Tree-creeper. Once seen running along the garden wall, when it was shot. There are scarcely any trees on Rathlin.

M. melanope, Pallas.—Grey Wagtail. Uncommon; one was cauglit alive in the summer of 1858, having flown into one of the rooms through an open window. I have reason to think they breed, as I found a pair at Alley Lough, in June, 1889, whose movements were suspicious, but I failed to find the nest.

*Anttius pratensis, L.—Meadow-pipit. Not uncommon; some nests with eggs have been found on some of the heath-covered hills, chiefly in the centre of the island. Several birds were found dead in the hard frost of January, 1867.

*A obscurus, Latham.—Rock-pipit. Common along the shore. Nests have been found in the heaps of dried seaweed stacked for making kelp.

*Muscicapa grisola, L.—Spotted Flycatcher. Is usually seen in summer, but the nest was never found till June, 1890, when a pair had a nest in a rose-tree against the wall of a greenhouse. The hen was very fearless.

***Hirundo rustica**, L.—Swallow. Common in summer; builds in outhouses and sheds. I observed it only about Mr. Gage's house and over the lakes. Has been seen on the 18th April (Migration Report, 1885).

***Chelidon urbica**, L.-House-martin. Very common in summer, more numerous than the last; builds in the White Rocks at the north side of Church Bay, in company with the Swift.

***Ligurinus chioris**, L.—Greenfinch. Numerous in winter; a nest was found for the first time in May, 1885.

Carduelis elegans, Stephens. Goldfinch. A winter visitor. Formerly, when brambles and wild roses were more plentiful, they bred regularly.

***Passer domesticus**, L.—House-sparrow. Common at all the farmhouses. I noticed that all I saw were distinctly lighter in colour and appeared also smaller than those on the mainland.

Fringilla coelebs, L.—Chaffinch. A few have been occasionally seen in the garden, but they have not been known to breed; chiefly seen in winter I did not observe any in the month of June.

***Acanthis cannabina**, L.—Linnet. Common in summer and winter; it breeds in low bushes and whins. Frequently observed by the light-keepers on migration.

[Mr. Howard Saunders, in the article referred to, mentions the Lesser Redpoll, **Acanthis rufescens**, Vieillot, as breeding on the island, but Mr. Gage states it is quite unknown.]

*A **flavii-ostris**, L—Twite. Fairly common all over the island, breeding in the higher ground. Mr. Howard Saunders found the nest on the ledge of a high cliff.

***Emberiza miliaria,** L.--Corn-bunting. Common and permanently resident; breeds in suitable localities.

*E. citrinella, L.—Yellow-bunting. More numerous than the last, and resident. Nests frequently found.

*E. scfroenicius, L.—Reed-bunting. Common in the bogs throughout the island, where it breeds.

Plectrophenax nevalis, L.—Snow-bunting. A regular winter visitant, sometimes in large flocks. Frequently seen on migration, as the following notes from the Reports will show ;"May 16th, shot a bird very like a Snow-bunting. October 14th, thirty. Some seen also on 15th, 17th, and 18th (October, 1883). October 16th, ten at noon, remain (1884). March 10th, one seen. September 6th, five going S."

*Sturnus vulgaris, L—Starling. Very common; it breeds in clefts of rocks, chiefly in the neighbourhood of Church Bay. Large flocks frequently observed on migration.

*Pyrrhocorax graculus, L.—Chough. Very common all over the island; they breed in the cliffs, chiefly at the White Rocks. Called "Jackdaw by the natives.

*Pica rustica, Scop.—Magpie. Not so frequently seen as formerly. They used to build in a clump of trees near Mr. Gage's house, but on some sportsmen shooting into the nests, they took to the rocks, where a few pairs still breed.

Corvus monedula, L.—Jackdaw. Rarely seen; occasionally comes from mainland.

*C. corax, L.—Raven. One or two pairs breed in the most inaccessible cliffs on the north side of the island; formerly they were much more numerous, and were very destructive to young lambs, etc. One bird was seen to pick the eyes out of a ewe just after lambing, and was shot by the shepherd. The latter—a very observant man—states that every year, as soon as the young birds were able to fly and procure their own food, the old birds regularly drove them away from the place. Both old and young birds would disappear from the island for four or five days, and then the old birds would return alone. In May, 1867, a singular fight between Peregrines and Ravens occurred. Both birds had nests at no great distance from each other, on a very inaccessible cliff. The Peregrine's eggs were wanted by a collector, and some boys, watching the birds away from the nest, went down on a rope, and took the eggs. The birds on their return, finding their nests empty, attacked the Ravens, killed the hen, and demolished the nest. The cock Raven fought fiercely, but was at last overcome by the Peregrines, who forsook that particular locality, and never returned. Up to this time both families had lived in apparent friendship, not interfering with each other, but it-was evident the Ravens were blamed for the theft. The fight was witnessed from the top of the cliffs by many who were attracted by the cries of the birds, and they described it as being most bloody and determined.

*Corvus cornix, L.—Hooded Crow. Very common; frequents the

beach of Church Bay and elsewhere. Breeds in
the cliffs.

C. frugilegus, L.- Rook. Young and old
birds sometimes seen in autumn and winter. Observed by light-
keepers on migration.

***Aiauda arvensis**, L.—Skylark. Common on the higher grounds, where
it breeds; frequently killed at the light-house in autumn.

***Cypselus apus**, L.—Swift. Common in summer. They breed in the
church tower, and also on the White Rocks at the N. side of Church
Bay, in company with the House-Martins.

Caprimulgus europoeus, L.—Nightjar. The only known occurrence
was in June, 1850, when a specimen was shot.

***Cucuius canorus**, L.—Cuckoo. A constant summer visitor. A young
bird, recently fledged, was found in a deserted nest in August, 1883.
Frequently observed by light-keepers; earliest date noted, April
20th.

Strix flammea, L.—Barn-owl. Formerly known as resident and
breeding in holes in the rocks; now very rarely seen.

Asio oius, L.—- Long-eared Owl. Very rare; one was shot 14th June,
1853, and another was caught alive in April, 1863.

A. accipitrinus, Pallas.—Short-eared Owl. Has once occurred, in
November, 1879, when a fine specimen was shot.

Circus aeruginosus, L.—Marsh-Harrier, Seen by the late R. Gage
12th June, 1867, searching for prey in one of the marshes at the west
end of the island. A bird supposed to be of this species was seen by
several people in the autumn of 1891.

Buteo vulgaris, Leach.—Common Buzzard. One was caught alive
with a broken wing below the cliffs on the north side, 28th February,
1845. Another was found dead in March, 1879. These are the only
known occurrences.

Haliaetus albicilla, L.—Sea Eagle. This bird was formerly a constant
resident, and bred in the rocks on the north side of the island, but
owing to the havoc it committed on young lambs it was shot down
and the nests robbed. It has not been seen for some years. Thompson,
writing in 1849, says "In the island of Rathlin the Sea-Eagle is said
to have an eyrie."I have not been able to find the date of the last
attempt to breed.

Accipiter nisus, L.—Sparrow-Hawk. Occasionally seen following
small birds. In October, 1867, one was seen by the land-steward
pursuing a thrush, which it followed into his kitchen, breaking a pane
of glass in the window.

Falco islandus, Gmelin.—Iceland Falcon. A fine specimen was seen
hovering over a sheep farm, and was shot by the shepherd, on March
9th, 1865. Its extreme length was 20 inches.

F. peregrinus, Tunstall. Peregrine Falcon. A constant resident, breeding in the cliffs at the north side of the island. Two pairs are known to breed regularly there.

F. aesalon, Tunstall.—-Merlin. The only occurrence of this little falcon was on the 10th December, 1888, when one was caught alive in a house into which it had pursued a bird.

F. tinnunculus, L.—Kestrel. Very common; breeds on cliffs all round the island. On the 2nd June, 1889, my cousin, Mr. Praeger, took a curious clutch of four eggs. They were white, mottled very slightly with reddish-brown, and the texture was exceedingly rough.

Phalacrocorax carbo, L.—Cormorant. Once very common at the Bull Rock, where they bred in the caves. They are only occasionally seen now, and have ceased to breed. An unusually large one taken alive in 1867, disgorged a Wrasse 14 inches long, 10 inches in girth, and 2 lbs. weight.

*P. graculus, L.—Shag. Very common, and breeds regularly in the caves near the Bull Rock; also at the north side of the island.

Sula bassana, L.—Gannet. Often seen fishing about the island during the autumn, and frequently reported by the fight- keepers. Young birds have been picked up on the beach after storms, and I observed adults flying over the island in June.

Ardea cinerea, L.—Common Heron. Many frequent the shores and reedy marshes, where small eels abound. Some of the inhabitants say they breed on the island, but Mr. Gage never saw a nest.

Anser cinereus, Meyer.—Grey Lag-Goose. Only seen in hard winters. One was shot in a field in October, 1867, and an adult female, weighing 8 lbs., was shot in January, 1867, on one of the loughs.

A. albifrons, Scopoli.—White-fronted Goose. Has been seen in the bay, near the shore, although a specimen has not yet been obtained. A single bird was observed in November, 1891.

A. segetum, Gmelin.—Bean Goose. Frequently seen in winter, and specimens have been procured at different times.

Bernicia leucopsis, Bechst.—Barnacle Goose. Has once occurred, one being shot on Ushet Lough, 30th January, 1868.

B. brenta, Pallas.—Brent Goose. Often seen in winter, sometimes in large flocks, and specimens have been secured.

Cygnus musicus, Bechst.—Whooper Swan. Rare; one was shot on Ushet Lough in February, 1848, and two others seen. A flock of 25 was seen in Church Bay in December, 1875. They were very wild, and being followed by Mr. Gage in a boat, they all went away in a westward direction.

C. bewicki, Tar.- -Bewick's Swan. Not uncommon in winter on the rocks, north and south. Two were shot on Claggan Lough, 22nd November, 1882, and another on Ushet at the same time, out of a flock of seven.

[A Black Swan, G. atratus, was shot by the Rev. G. M'Lean on one of the loughs about the centre of the island, on the 23rd

November, 1883.]

Tados-na cornufa, Gmelin.—Common Sheldrake. Often seen in winter, and specimens have been frequently shot in the autumn. In the *Migration Report* for 1882, the light-keeper reports that the Sheldrake breeds on the island, but Mr. Gage does not mention the fact, and my enquiries tend to prove that it does not breed.

*****Anas boscas,** L—Wild Duck. Very common, and breeds in every suitable place. I obtained a clutch of seven very pale buff eggs on the island.

*****Querquedula crecca**, L.—Teal. Common, and breeds in moderate numbers.

Mareca penelope, L.—Wigeon. Common on the large loughs in winter, and in Church Bay.

Fuliguia ferina, L.—Pochard. Common winter visitor to the loughs, and frequently shot,

F. cristata, Leach.—Tufted Duck. Fairly common among the other clucks in winter.

F. mariia, L.~Scaup. Very common in winter in Church Bay, and not often seen in the loughs; but in May, 1865, a mature male in breeding plumage was shot on "Ushet Lough.

Clangula glacion, L.— Golden-eye. Common in Church Bay in the winter months, but never seen on the island.

Hareida glacialis, L.~Long-tailed Duck. Immature birds are not uncommon in Church Bay in the autumn and winter months. A fine male in full plumage was shot in November, 1863.

Somatena mollissima, L— Eider Duck. Not unfrequently seen in winter, Four came into Ushet port, 13th September, 1870, and one—a young male—was secured. A male in fine mature plumage was shot at the east side, 17th May, 1872, and on the 10th November, 1877, a female was shot on the strand. An adult male was seen in Church Bay, 16th November, 1882, and was followed without success. They are more often seen at the east and south sides of the island, and when they depart it is always in an eastward direction. Females are more commonly seen than males. "April 3rd, three Eider Duck drifting W. 16th, seventeen Eider Duck on the water."(*. Migration Report,* 1886, page 173).

S. pectabilis, L.—King-Eider. Has once occurred. A female was shot in a bay, west of Church Point, in November, 1861, and was sent to Mr. Howard Saunders for identification.

Aedemia nigra, L. Common Scoter. Not at all common. A female was shot near the light-house, in November, 1869, and a mature male was shot in Ushet port in March, 1873.

Mergus merganser, L.—Goosander. Very rare; two females were shot near the west end of the island in January, 1877, and another female at Ushet port in January, 1878.

M. serrator, L—Red-breasted Merganser. Often seen fishing in Church

Bay, and specimens have been shot.

*Columba livia, Gmelin.—Rock-Dove. Very common, and breeds in considerable numbers at the White Rocks.

Phasinus colchicus, L.—Pheasant.—Has several times been observed on the island at long intervals, but no specimen has yet been secured.

Perdix cinerea, Latham.—Partridge. Is never seen except in very hard weather; last occurrence, December, 1878.

Coturnix communis, Bonn—Quail. Has occasionally been met with. One was shot in December, 1846, and another in January, 1867,

*Crex pratensis, Bechst.——Corn Crake. Common in the meadows and cornfields, where it breeds. Earliest date heard, April 27th.

*Rallus aquaticus, L.~Water-Rail. Frequent in the marshes, where it breeds.

*Gallinula chloropus, L.—Water-Hen. Very common in all the loughs, where it breeds.

*Fulica atra, L.—Coot. Very common, and breeds in large numbers.

*Aegialitis hiaticula, L.—Ringed Plover. Often seen about the strand and rocks. An unfledged bird was found in July, 1874, and I observed a pair in June, 1889, evidently nesting.

Charadrius pluviaius, L.—Golden Plover. Frequents the beach in hard winters.

*Vanellus vulgaris, Bechst.—Lapwing. Common in summer on the bogs, where it breeds; not so numerous in winter.

Strepsilas interpres, L.---Turnstone. Frequently seen, both in winter and summer plumage.

*Haematopus ostralegus, L.—Oyster-catcher. A few pairs are permanently resident, and breed in several places along the shore.

Phalaropus fulicarius, L.—Grey Phalarope. Has been occasionally seen swimming in Church Bay, and specimens have been shot.

Scolopax rusticula, L.—Woodcock. Only seen in severe weather; has been several times shot in winter.

Gallinago coelestis, Frenzel.—Common Snipe. Abundant in all the bogs, where it breeds.

G. gallinula, L.-- Jack Snipe. Fairly common in winter, and observed by the light-keepers as sometimes striking against the lantern.

Tringa alpina, L.—Dunlin. Frequent on the reefy shores about Church Bay in spring and summer. One in the late Mr. Gage's collection is in full breeding plumage, and I should not be surprised if this species were found breeding on the island.

T. striata, L.——Purple Sandpiper. Seen every winter in limited numbers.

Tringa Canutes, L.—Knot. Sometimes seen, but not at all common.

Calidris arenaria, L.—Sanderling. Has once occurred, a specimen being shot in Church Bay, 2nd March, 1862.

*Totanus hypoleucus, L.—Common Sandpiper. Breeds in small numbers on the island.

T. calidris, Common Redshank. Frequent in winter; one was shot in August, 1844.

Numenius arquata, L.—Curlew. Frequent along the shore in winter and spring.

N. phaeopus, L.—Whiinbrel. Seen in small numbers every spring.

Sterna dougalli, Montagu.—Roseate Tern. Sometimes seen, but not nearly so frequently of late years. A fine specimen was shot in March, 1841—a very remarkable date.

S. fiuviatilis, Naumann.—Common Tern. Often seen in summer along the shore.

S. macrura, Naumann.—Arctic Tern. As the preceding, but not so numerous. One was caught alive in a field, October, 1860.

Larus ridibundus, L.—Black-headed Gull. In winter months this gull is found in great numbers, but is never seen in summer.

L. canus, L.—Common Gull. Very rarely seen; a bird in first year's plumage was shot in January, 1860.

*__**L. argentatus**__, Gmelin.—Herring-Gull. Very common, and breeds in large numbers.

*__**L. fuscus**__, L.—Lesser Black-backed Gull. A few pairs breed at the north side of the island every year.

L. marinus, L.—Great Black-backed Gull. Occasionally seen in winter, and specimens have been shot.

L. glaucus, Fab.—Glaucous Gull. An immature bird was shot in February, 1867, and another in February, 1869. Since then they have been occasionally seen. A fine adult bird, in beautiful plumage, was caught alive in a net, 9th October, 1891.

*__**Rissa tridactyla**__, L.—Kittiwake Gull. Immense numbers breed at the Bull Rock and at the north side.

Stercorarius pomatorhinus, Temm.—Pomatorhine Skua. Not uncommonly seen on the pasture lands in autumn and winter. An immature bird was captured alive in a field, 22nd October, 1891.

S. crepidatus, Gmelin.—Richardson's Skua. Young birds are frequently seen, and have been shot. An adult was captured alive in September, 1886.

S. parasiticus, L.—Buffon's Skua. A fine specimen in perfect plumage was taken alive at Ballygill, in May, 1860. Three others were seen at the same time.

*__**Alco torda**__, L. -Razor-bill.

*__**Uria triole**__, L.—Common Guillemot

Countless numbers of both species breed on the western and northern cliffs every year. The variety known as the Binged Guillemot is very common.

*__**U. grylle**__, L.—Black Guillemot. Breeds in moderate numbers on the cliffs, and remains all the year.

Merguius aile, L.~Little Auk. Occasionally seen. In December, 1862, three were picked up dead. One was caught alive on the high road in

January, 1863, and since then a few have been found dead on the beach at intervals.

***Fratercula arctica**, L.—Puffin. Breeds in large numbers on the grassy slopes, usually arriving about 17th March.

Colymbus glacialis, L.—Great Northern Diver. Occasionally seen in Church Bay, and has been shot in summer plumage. Two were seen in June, 1885.

C. septentrionalis, L.—Red - throated Diver. Sometimes seen. One was shot on Ushet Lough in the winter of 1868.

Podicipes auritus, L.—Sclavonian Grebe. Has once occurred, in December, 1871.

***P. fluviatilis**, Tunstall. Little Grebe. Common in the marshes, where it breeds,

Fulmarus glacialis, L.—Fulmar Petrel. The only specimen seen was captured .alive on the rocks near the light-house, 2nd September, 1889. It was an adult in good plumage.

***Puffinus anglorum**, Temm.—Manx Shearwater. Common on the north side of the island, where it breeds.

Cymochorea leucorrhoa, Vieillot.—Fork-tailed Petrel. After the storms of November, 1881, and October, 1891, several specimens were picked up dead on the beach.

roceilaria pelagica, L.—Storm Petrel. Often seen flying over the sea, and is commonly found on the beach after storms. It is said by the light-keepers to breed on the island, but Mr. Gage never found it, and I think it has been confused with the Manx Shearwater.

See also ;—Notes on the present status of birds on Rathlin Island, by G. F. Mitchell—*Irish Naturalists' Journal,* Vol. IX, No. 2. April, 1947.

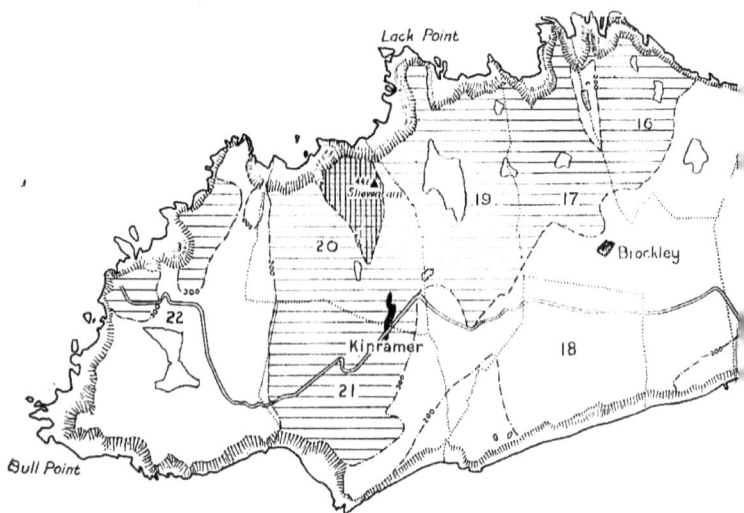

Lack Point

Slievard

Brockley

Kinramer

Bull Point

R A T H L I N   S O U N D

TOWNLANDS

1.	Roonivoolin.
2.	Carravindoon.
3.	Carravinally.
4.	Kinkeel.
5.	Craigmacagan.
6.	Demesne.
7	Ballynoe.
8.	Glebe
9.	Ballycarry.
10	Mullindress.
11	Church Quarter.
12	Ballyconagan.
13	Ballynagard.
14	Kilpatrick.
15	Knockans
16	Ballygill N.
17	Ballygill M.
18	Ballygill S.
19	Cleggan
20	Kinramer N.
21	Kinramer S.
22	Kebhle

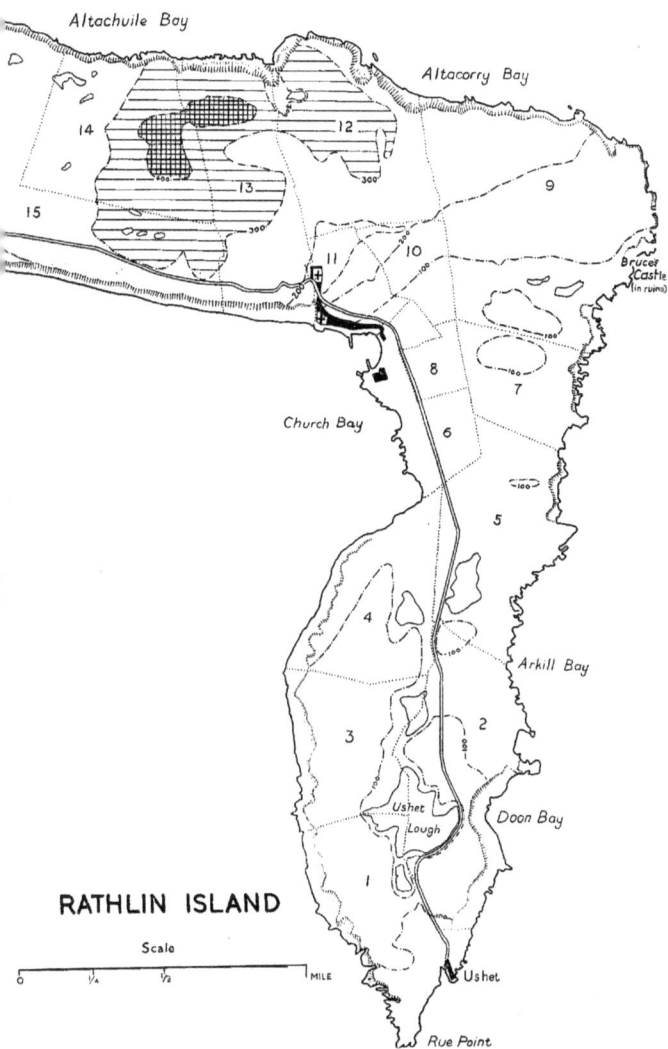

Altachuile Bay

Altacorry Bay

14

12

13

15

9

Brucel
Castle
(in ruins)

11

10

8

7

Church Bay

6

5

Arkill Bay

4

2

3

Ushet
Lough

Doon Bay

1

RATHLIN ISLAND

Scale

0   1/4   1/2   MILE

Ushet

Rue Point

Clachan
Publishing

clachanpublishing.com

We are a small, niche publishing company,
that specialises in short-run editions of
family and local histories, local interest publications, poetry,
and the like.
We also publish modern editions of antiquarian books.
These are carefully formatted and edited to modern standards.
Our publications are available on our website:
https://www.clachanbooks.com

www.ingramcontent.com/pod-product-compliance
Lightning Source LLC
LaVergne TN
LVHW051757080426
835511LV00018B/3341